# Trust also in Him

## The True Story of a Life Woven by God

To Peggy Bryan
with love!
Emily Potter
Is. 40:31
2015

# *Trust also in Him*
## The True Story of a Life Woven by God

"Commit thy way unto the Lord;
trust also in Him,
and He shall bring it to pass."
Psalm 37:5

By Emily Potter
S.D.G.
*Soli Deo Gloria*

Photo credits:

Pages 21, 69, 152, 157, and 158: courtesy of the Bundesarchiv via
Wikimedia Commons, under the Creative Commons Attribution-Share
Alike 3.0 License.

Page 30: Photo by Richard Peter, courtesy of Deutsche Fotothek via
Wikimedia Commons, under the Creative Commons Attribution-Share
Alike 3.0 License.

Page 25: Detail from watercolor by Friedrich Wilhelm Moritz, courtesy
of the Swiss National Library, *GS-GUGE-MORITZ-C-2,* via
Wikimedia Commons. Public domain.

Page 35: Photo courtesy of Mr. and Mrs. Armin Blischke.

Pages 146, 201, and 208: Photos by Emily Potter.

All other photographs and documents from the private collection of
Mrs. Elisabeth Blischke.

All scripture quotations taken from the King James Version of
the Bible.

# Contents

# Acknowledgments

The "firstfruits" of my gratitude are offered with joy to my Savior and King, who made each step of this writing possible. The truth of His word, "Without Me ye can do nothing," and its beautiful counterpart, "I can do all things through Christ which strengtheneth me," were marvelously evident over the past seven years. For the gift of His Spirit to guide, counsel, and inspire, I can never praise Him enough, but oh, the joy of knowing that because of Jesus' blood I can spend eternity trying!

Many thanks to my church family and the many other friends who faithfully prayed for me. The part you played in the book may never be known on earth, but may you find those prayers again one day as gold that survives the fire.

Thank you to all those who were willing to proofread and edit the manuscript, particularly Mrs. Laura Sporre, Miss Krystal Nisly, Mrs. Michelle Lane, and my grandfather, Mr. Ronald Potter. Your encouragement and insight were invaluable.

Special thanks to Mrs. Pamela Caldwell for her editing advice and encouragement.

Heartfelt thanks to Mr. and Mrs. Armin Blischke for answering my many questions, checking and rechecking the manuscript, and welcoming me into their home as one of the family. Your warmth and hospitality were a blessing from the Lord, and I cherish your continued friendship and prayers.

A tremendous thank you to my family for their patience, prayers, and support throughout this project. Special thanks to my brothers Timothy and Daniel for unraveling the mystery of knitting *paschke*, and to them and my mother for helping me knit samples and adjust the pattern.

To my parents, who have faithfully taught, trained, and loved me for the last thirty years, I owe an incalculable debt of gratitude. For your prayers, wisdom, counsel, generosity, and love, I thank you more than I can say. May your loving care for one of the "least of these" find a sure reward on the last day.

*"Now to Him who is able to keep you from falling, and to present you faultless before the presence of His glory with exceeding joy, to the only wise God our Saviour, be glory and majesty, dominion and power, both now and ever. Amen."* (Jude 24-25).

# Preface

Seven years ago the Lord gave me a desire to chronicle His work in the world today. Conversations with the older generation had long been one of my joys. I loved their stories of things they had seen and lessons they had learned. I especially enjoyed talking to older Christians. I *know* that God is faithful; they have *seen* that He is faithful. I longed to write down their stories of what the Lord had done. Many of my friends were in their eighties or nineties; if left unwritten, their stories would soon disappear. I wanted the church to have the encouragement of seeing the Lord prove Himself true in life after life, and most of all I wanted the Lord to have the glory He deserved for His work.

With that goal in mind, I pursued several opportunities for writing biographies, but the Lord closed the doors in various ways. I wrote a number of short biographies of older members of the church for our church newsletter, and learned how hard it is to condense someone's life into 700 words!

One Sunday a sweet, smiling lady with a German accent whom I knew as Mrs. Blischke came up to me at church. She liked the way I had written two of her friends' stories for the newsletter, and wanted me to write down her whole story. I was thrilled.

I knew Mr. and Mrs. Blischke by name and enjoyed brief conversations with them on Sundays, but they were about to become some of my closest friends. I visited them in their home, and spent a wonderful afternoon hearing what the Lord had done in their lives. I wrote a newsletter article from that first interview, and it was impossible to get those two lives into my allotted word count. I called the editor.

"I've got it down to 900 words, and if I take out much more it's just going to be a list of facts," I said.

The editor suggested we split the story into two parts, and after the newsletter came out a number of people at church were upset with me. They didn't want to wait for the next issue to find out what happened!

Work on the book went slowly at first. The language difference made asking and answering questions difficult, but after the Blischkes had a discussion in German one of them usually thought of the right word in English. Many of the more obscure words I was able to guess from their hand motions. It helped that my family loves old farming tools and methods.

After three interviews, the Blischkes' health problems put the book on hold for more than two years. I wrote what I could, but there were so many unanswered questions that a cohesive story was close to impossible.

In May, 2012, Mr. Blischke went home to be with the Lord. I had prayed in faith that the Lord would allow him to live until I could write his story down, and I couldn't understand why the Lord had taken him.

That December, Mrs. Blischke moved to Brookfield, Wisconsin, to be close to family. The language difference hadn't been too bad when we could use our hands and facial expressions, but over the phone it was far more difficult. I prayed about going to visit, and left it in the Lord's hands. We kept in touch by mail and phone, and during that time she asked me to start calling her Elisabeth. Oh, that was hard! She had been "Mrs. Blischke" in my mind for so long, except in the book, that I often stumbled a bit before I said "Elisabeth" on the phone.

On December 30, 2013, almost exactly one year after Elisabeth moved, my grandfather called. He had an airline rewards ticket expiring in three weeks, and asked if anyone at our house would like to take a trip. My dad and I prayed about it that night, and the Lord's answer was clear: "Go." Three weeks later, on January 15, 2014, I left for Brookfield.

That snowy week in Wisconsin was a wonderful time. Mrs. Blischke and I prayed together, read the Bible together, walked together, and just plain *talked*. It was the first time we'd had more than an afternoon to talk, and story after story, with the details that make a book come alive, flowed from those conversations. We went carefully over what I had written, correcting misunderstandings and adding fascinating snapshots of life in a time that vanished long before many of us were born. Despite her years as a refugee, Elisabeth had saved almost everything—pictures, postcards, documents—and I lugged a scanner along to scan them into a laptop. She showed me her little German Bible, and I noted down verses she had marked.

After I got home, I started completely rewriting my manuscript. The book more than doubled in length, and far more than doubled in quality and power. With more knowledge of dates and places, I researched the historical context of the stories, clearing up many questions and adding unexpected historical value to the story. I prayed constantly that the Lord would guide my words. I wanted the story to be true, not just in facts, but in the "feel" of the way Mrs. Blischke told it. Most of all, I wanted the Lord's work to shine through, undimmed by faults in my writing.

I knew I would have to go back to Wisconsin before publishing the book. There were enough misunderstandings in the first manuscript that I couldn't trust the new stories without double-checking them. The Lord provided money for a ticket, and I hoped to go back in May for Elisabeth's 85th birthday. When I e-mailed her sister-in-law (also Elisabeth Blischke), she said Elisabeth was expecting company through the summer and the best time to come would be in the fall. I was disappointed to put if off so long, but I've learned by experience that my Lord's timing is perfect, so I waited.

In the meantime, the Lord gave me other uses for some of the money I had saved up. One day He gave me a specific amount to use as He led. I went to my little stash, and the money that was left was the amount He had told me, to the dollar. That was exciting, and to have to truly trust the Lord for money was exciting, too. Then I remembered the trip to Wisconsin, and suddenly trusting the Lord seemed a lot less exciting. I had told Elisabeth the Lord had provided money for the trip, and He had, but now He'd had me use it for something else. I knew—missionary biographies are my favorite reading material—that the Lord can bring money from totally unexpected sources with pinpoint timing. The only problem was, I didn't know of any unexpected source for the Lord to use.

Just a few weeks later, not knowing the extent of my lack of funds, my mom told me that she and my dad had decided to give me the trip to Wisconsin for my birthday. That was far beyond any birthday present our family usually gave. It was my Lord simply sweeping the money problem out of the way. On my birthday morning I found tickets on sale, and left for Wisconsin on September 29.

During the visit Elisabeth and I meticulously checked and rechecked the book. At first she was hesitant to tell me anything was wrong, so I took to watching her expression. If she looked at all confused or surprised, I stopped and asked what was wrong. Anything I wasn't sure about I read again, or rephrased it to make sure she understood the English words. There were fewer mistakes than I expected.

When we finished the last page, Elisabeth said, "I could *see* it happening as you read." All my prayers and my agonizing over word choices were rewarded by that incredible sentence. Somehow the Lord overruled my errors, and the story was true—as I had prayed so often—not just in fact but in feeling.

The next month was full of working in the changes, and in November I sent the manuscript to friends who were helping me edit. The editing improved the manuscript tremendously, and I spent the editing time resampling and restoring the old photographs, many of which were in bad shape from the hard refugee years. The Lord guided every step, and I praise Him for His goodness and grace.

I dreamed of taking the finished book to Wisconsin in person, but funds were a decidedly limiting factor. One morning I asked the Lord to provide money for whatever He wanted me to do. If the money came, I would go. If it didn't, I would take that as my Lord's leading. That afternoon an elderly friend called. His wife was in poor health, and he wanted to hire me to help them in the evenings. At first I thought I wouldn't take money just for visiting friends, but the Lord reminded me of my prayer that morning. I told our friend about my prayer, and said that if he wanted to pay me, that would be the Lord's answer. They needed my help for a week and a half, and their generosity provided just over what I needed for the trip to Brookfield. Lord willing, I will leave next month with the printed book in hand.

Mrs. Blischke and I prayed many times—together and apart—for the Lord to use her story for His glory. We prayed for those who would read it, too, that the Lord would turn many to Himself through the book.

As the Lord has blessed the writing, may He now bless the reading of His marvelous work as the Master Weaver. He is the same God today, and all who trust in Him will still find Him absolutely faithful.

Emily Potter
Altadena, 2015

# God Sits A-Weaving

## Gott sitzt am Webstuhl meines Lebens

Words and Melody - Traditional German
English Translation and Harmony by Emily Potter

1.God sits a - weav - ing at my life-loom; He holds the threads with - in His hand,
2.Though man - y rough threads He al - low-eth, They pass through His dear Fath - er - hand,
3.Yet on the loom I still am peace-ful, When threads He spins are dark and sad.
4.And when the last day, as God will - eth, My dy - ing day, shall pass a - way,

And not in vain He crafts the pat - tern, to make it please Him strand by strand.
And He through all for me pre - par - eth A robe of light for Heav - en's land.
I fix my eyes on one pure gold thread, And like a child, my heart is glad.
Then is the loom spun off; all shin - eth, Like pur-est gold, with heav'n - ly ray.

Though strange to me it some times seemeth, When so con - fused the threads He plies,
And al - so threads dark, dim and som ber, In - to my cloth the Wea - ver plaits.
For wheth - er all is light or darkness, In ev' - ry - thing there still gleams bright
Then sing I with the an - gel chor-us, With the last night of bat - tle won,

His hand will nev - er sink or fal - ter, While He the weav-er's shut - tle guides.
These are life's cloud - ed, dim, bleak hou - rs, When I for Him in si - lence wait.
The gold - en thread of love so might y, That chose me as His child of light.
To hon - or my great Mas - ter Weav - er, "Yes, tru - ly Thou hast all well done."

# 1

## *November, 1944*

It was Sunday morning. Nestled in a tree-filled valley, the little Hungarian town of Szárazd[1] lay deceptively quiet. The Alpen church steeple calmly overlooked the brown tile roofs. A Slavic melody wafted through the air. Beyond the rolling hills, the waters of the great Danube River flowed by undisturbed. Nothing in that peaceful scene gave a hint of one young girl's grief as she walked for the last time through the farmhouse she loved. For Elisabeth Winecker,[2] that cold autumn morning was dark with the clouds of war and the threat of an unknown future.

Elisabeth walked through each familiar door and looked around each room. She had been so happy here! There was the bedroom, scene of hilarious, surreptitious romps with her two younger brothers after Father tucked them in bed. Now Father was in Yugoslavia with the army, and the bedroom was lonely and deserted. Mother's beautiful furniture still stood regally in the "good room." The

---

1  Hungarian, pronounced sahr'-ahzd
2  German, vin'-ə-ker

green plush couch with the red roses looked just as it had last summer when Elisabeth had appendicitis and Father sent her in from the field to lie down there and rest. She would never forget that couch! Mother's cook-stove in the kitchen, the spicy-smelling smokehouse, the family table...so many stories, so many memories.

Elisabeth had been born in this house, with its thick, hand-stamped clay walls. Here her father, grandfather, and great-grandfather had lived and worked, farming the land to make a life for their families. It had been a good life, and now, as she turned from it, she had no way of knowing the bitter struggles that lay ahead. As she closed the farmhouse door, she embarked on a journey the Lord had planned for her since the beginning of time; an impossible journey that would take her across Europe and halfway around the world. Trials and heartaches lay unseen in the future, but with each step God, the Master Weaver, was drawing together the threads of a story so intricate that only He could have conceived it.

*"One generation shall praise Thy works to another, and shall declare Thy mighty acts." (Psalm 145:4).*

As the Weaver added the thread of that dark November Sunday to Elisabeth's life, He was setting the pattern for a tapestry that richly deserves to be displayed to generations to come.

\*     \*     \*     \*     \*     \*     \*

*A lovely view of Szárazd from the cornfield on the Wineckers' hill.*

The first threads of the tapestry were spun in Hungary, long before Elisabeth was born. Elisabeth's *opa*,[3] or grandfather, lived and was married in pretty little Szárazd. The Lord gave Johann Winecker and his wife three daughters. Johann was an orderly man, even by the stringent standards of Szárazd. He had the distinction of owning the first toothbrush in the village.

A team of two horses helped Johann on the Winecker farm. Farm animals were almost like members of the family in Szárazd, and the horses' names, Gesar and Lenyel, hung over their stalls in the barn. Many years later, after the horses and their owner were gone, Johann's granddaughter would look

---

3   oh'-pah

curiously at the two names still hanging over the stalls.

The Winecker farm was a small one, but its thirteen acres were enough to keep the farmer and his horses busy and to produce a range of crops that supplied nearly all the family's needs.

Then sorrow came to the farm. Johann's wife died, and he and the girls were left alone. After some time, Johann met a young lady named Katharina Lepp.[4] Katharina, Elisabeth's *oma*,[5] was born in neighboring Felsőnána[6] in 1881. Katharina and Johann were married, and in 1905 God gave them a son. In Szárazd's strongly traditional society, the oldest son was customarily named after his father, so the Wineckers christened this little one Johann. In 1909, God added a little sister. Annamarie, called Anna, completed the Winecker family.

On June 28, 1914, far away from quiet Szárazd, a man was killed on the streets of Sarajevo. His death touched off the "powderkeg of Europe," and the explosion enveloped the farmers of Szárazd and the entire world. One month after the assassination of Archduke Francis Ferdinand, Austria-Hungary declared war on Serbia. Johann was among the thousands of young men sent by the emperor into the Balkans as World War I began.

The invasion of Serbia was a disaster. In the first five months of the war, the imperial army lost

---

4   kaht-ah-ree'-na lepp
5   oh'-mah
6   fel-shə-nah'-na; a village about twelve miles from Szárazd

227,000 of the 450,000 troops engaged in the campaign. Johann was among those who never returned. Along with so many of the flower of the Austro-Hungarian Empire, he was buried in one of the fierce little countries that after the war were called simply Yugoslavia. The "war to end all wars," the conflict was optimistically called, but the seeds of injustice and discontent planted at Versailles were taking root. Less than thirty years later, Johann's son would follow him down to Yugoslavia, caught in a struggle more brutal, more destructive than the first. Little Johann was nine years old when his father died. He tried to take over the work of the farm, but the burden was too heavy for a child to shoulder. His opa was elderly now, and unable to manage the physical labor the horses required. Johann did his best, cleaning the horses' stalls before he left for school, but soon Gesar and Lenyel had to be sold. The beloved horses were exchanged for cows, and a less demanding method of farming.

Johann's time was divided between farm work and school. Despite the heavy workload, he excelled in his studies. The children were graded by a system of marks: *kitűnő*,[7] "outstanding," *jeles*,[8] "excellent," *jó*,[9] "good," and so on. Johann was a diligent student, and his report card boasted many of the coveted *kitűnő* marks.

---

7   kit'-uh-nurh
8   yel'-esh
9   yoh

When the boy farmer grew into a young man, he found the girl he wanted to marry. Circumstances and tradition, however, rendered the marriage impossible. Johann was the Wineckers' only son, and as such his duty was to remain on the family farm. The young lady was her parents' only daughter, and to marry a man bound to his own land would leave them without a support in their old age. Johann had his responsibility, and she had hers. There was nothing more to be said, and there the matter ended.

Then Johann noticed Elisabeth Becht.[10] The petite, sweet-faced daughter of the town mayor was six years younger than himself. Difficulties stood in the way here as well, because her father was a wealthy man. He was a *bauer*,[11] a "high farmer," while the Wineckers, though not poor, were only "half farmers." In the eyes of Szárazd society, this was a formidable objection to the match. Nevertheless, Elisabeth was Johann's choice, and this time tradition bowed to the young farmer's hopes. The wedding was set for March, 1928.

The preparations and festivities of a Szárazd wedding lasted six days. Each day had its own set task. On the first day the fine egg-noodles were rolled thin, cut, and laid out to dry. On another day the chickens were butchered, or, if the wedding was a large one, a calf. There was dense, rich *kuchen*,[12] traditional German cake, to be baked, and on the day

---

10 bekt
11 bow'-er
12 koo'-khen

before the wedding the friends of the bride borrowed silverware, tables, and other supplies for the wedding feast.

The bride and her family sewed the wedding costume. The traditional Szárazd wedding dress was almost completely black. The Bechts were wealthy, and Elisabeth's was fine silk. Two rows of small, round buttons ran down the front of the high-necked bodice, and narrow pleated ruffles ringed the cuffs of the long, fitted sleeves. The black *halztuch,*[13] or shawl, was ornamented with a heavy fringe almost a foot long. Dainty black cutwork embroidery, similar to eyelet lace, decorated the black apron. Scalloped points ran around the apron's edge, each holding a small five-petaled flower, and trios of larger cutwork flowers formed the corners of an inset floral border. Under the apron, the enormously full black skirt was held out by three or four stiffly starched petticoats. The curved, crown-like headdress was also black, thickly embroidered in bright colors and beaded with pearls. In her hand the bride carried a beautiful white handkerchief.

On the wedding day, the groom and guests formed a bright, festive procession as they marched through the streets of Szárazd to the bride's home. When they arrived in front of *Bauer* Becht's courtly house, they recited the traditional wedding poem ending, "Bring out to us the young bride!"

Elisabeth appeared in the doorway, giving Johann his first glimpse of his bride in her wedding

---

13 hahlz'-tookh

dress. She joined him at the head of the procession, and they led the way to the Lutheran church, where the marriage ceremony was performed. Johann's sister Anna and her fiancé were married beside them, doubling the wedding and the celebration. All then returned to the Winecker farm for the wedding feast, followed by traditional music and folk dancing.

It was a joyous day, and several of the young boys took advantage of the occasion to set a prank afoot. They took a pair of gold-rimmed spectacles belonging to a friend of the family and headed for the sheepfold. Their joke—an innocent sheep peering through the golden glasses—had short-lived success. The sheep bolted, taking the glasses with it. After a frantic search, sheep and spectacles were returned to their proper places by the crestfallen pranksters. Many years later, one of the perpetrators confessed to Johann and Elisabeth's daughter the part he played in her parents' celebration.

The day of the double wedding with its excitement and bustle over, the young farmer and his bride settled down happily to their new life together. Johann showed himself a good and diligent provider for his wife and for the little daughter the Lord brought them the next year. She was born on May 12, 1929, and they named her for her mother—Elisabeth.

# 2

## *A Seedling Grows*

*"The lines are fallen unto me in pleasant places;*
*yea, I have a goodly heritage."*

~*Psalm 16:6*[1]

Like the sprouting plants that nosed their way up through the Hungarian soil, Elisabeth spent her first years sending down roots and pushing her leaves toward the sun. Her world was bright and happy. The village was full of little friends to play with, and as the first grandchild on both sides, she was surrounded by the attention and love of a large extended family. In her parents, God gave the little seedling loving gardeners to watch and tend her as she grew.

Father was a strong, forthright man, a hard worker and skilled craftsman. He ruled his own character well, and taught his children to do the same. Obedience, respect for others, diligence, and perseverance were qualities that he insisted upon. A man of uncompromising integrity, Father's strictness

---

[1] The verses heading each chapter were taken from those marked by Elisabeth in her Bible.

*Little Elisabeth in front of her family's well.*

was tempered by a sincere love for his family. He was also a religious man who took his children's spiritual education seriously. From their earliest childhood he taught them to pray, and after more than half a century Elisabeth could still repeat the prayers she learned at his side.

Gentle and quiet, Mother was the perfect complement for Father. She passionately loved her children, and worked tirelessly for them. Although never strong, Mother kept up the heavy workload of a farm wife with quiet determination. In the midst of her many chores she still took time for her little ones. While she sat milking the cows, she called the children to bring their little enameled tin cups and filled them with fresh warm milk. Mother's dextrous fingers kept her family well-clothed and warm. Her love was shown in the beautifully made little dresses and suits that Elisabeth and her brothers wore, and in the small touches of beauty that she added to even the simplest articles of clothing.

In 1932, the first little brother arrived. Following Szárazd tradition, he was named Johann, but was always called by his nickname, Hans. The tradition of passing down first names made certain names—particularly Johann, Heinrich, Katharina, and Elisabeth—far more common than others, so

*Elisabeth and her younger brother Hans.*

*Oma Winecker with Heini and a cousin.*

everyone in Szárazd had nicknames. With the family
name first as Hungarian tradition dictated, Elisabeth
was known in the village as *Winecker Lisje,*[2] "Little
Elisabeth." Heinrich, nicknamed Heini,[3] was born in
1937. The boys joined Elisabeth as playmates and
fellow workers, and, like her, they thrived on the
hearty life of the farm.

---

2   liss'-ee-a
3   hine'-rick; hie'-nee

The farm was also home to Oma Winecker, left a widow after her husband's death in World War I. Like the other grandmothers of Szárazd, Oma did the lighter work of the farm while Mother helped Father in the fields. Oma tended the garden, cooked the meals, and watched the children as they played.

The Winecker farm was a wonderland for the children, from the crackling haymow to the cool, damp wine cellar. If young Elisabeth, running up to their drive from the village street, had stopped to take a long look around her home, she would have seen a pleasant picture of neatness and fruitfulness. On the left of the drive lay a large vegetable garden, and behind it the family drew water from their own well. Like David, who longed for the water of Bethlehem,[4] Elisabeth remembered no other water that tasted as good as a fresh, cold drink from that well.

On the right of the drive lay the low, white farmhouse, the heart of life on the farm. In front of the house, a wild rose bush spread its fragrance through the air, and tiny, pure white *Maiglöckchen,*[5] lilies of the valley, grew in springtime. Like the other homes in Szárazd, the sturdy clay walls of the farmhouse were built by hand. Elisabeth once watched Father help build a new house for their neighbors. The villagers used a method called

---

4   II Samuel 23:13-17
5   mie'-gluck-shen; "gluck" to rhyme with "book." Literally, "little bells of May."

rammed-earth construction. Wooden forms held the clay in place as the men raised the walls. The men shoveled clay into the wooden framework and then used tampers, heavy wooden cylinders on the end of long poles, to pound the clay into a compact mass. When the packed clay was dry, the forms were moved up and new layers of clay added until the walls reached the desired height. Almost a foot thick, the solid walls of the Wineckers' home kept the rooms cool in summer and warm in winter.

Under the roof of brown-gray handmade tiles, the rooms were laid out in a single row. The split Dutch door in the middle of the house swung open into the kitchen, full of the savory smells of Oma's cooking. On the right was the living room, which doubled as the sleeping room. Three narrow beds, raised high off the floor in Hungarian style, lined one wall. Hand-woven sheets and thick feather comforters were piled high above well-stuffed straw ticks. As a hen pulls each straw into place before settling down to brood, so a newly-stuffed tick required some shifting around before the prickles were smoothed down. Once Elisabeth had her "nest" in order, though, the straw was warm and comfortable.

Beside the beds stood a wooden chest that held one of the Wineckers' most treasured possessions: the massive family Bible. That Bible had an irresistible attraction for Elisabeth. As a small girl, she carefully lifted the huge book from its resting place and sat down to read. Like the boy

*The Wineckers' home in Szárazd, photographed after the war. The electric lines are a post-war innovation that replaced the oil lamps of Elisabeth's childhood.*

Samuel, Elisabeth "did not yet know the Lord,"[6] but the Word of the Lord was calling her as He called Samuel, even as a child. Years later, Elisabeth remembered reading Isaiah 53. It interested her, as it had the Ethiopian eunuch,[7] but years passed before she came to truly know the Lord Jesus the passage so beautifully described.

Above the chest, bars of light streamed through the shutter slats on the window. The shutters were open during the bright days of summer, and tightly closed in winter's cold. Between the next two windows stood the family table, and against the wall was Mother's sewing machine.

---

6   I Samuel 3:7
7   Acts 8:26-40

On the other side of the kitchen, to the left of the double front door, was the "good room." The counterpart of the early American parlor, the good room was filled with fine furniture and used only to entertain guests.

Next in line, the summer kitchen allowed Mother to cook in hot weather without heating the main rooms. Separated by a wall from the summer kitchen was the smokehouse—a round chimney filled with hanging rows of homemade sausages and hams. Under the chimney was the raised clay oven where Mother baked the crusty loaves Elisabeth loved. In another small room a ladder led to the attic, where the family stored grain and winter food supplies.

Tucked away in a row behind the house were the cow shed, the hayloft, and the storeroom for the plow and other farm tools. In the open space behind the house lay Father's new pigsty, with the corncrib conveniently nearby. On the other side of the drive behind the garden was a small barn for the sheep and chickens. A woodshed and a little wooden outhouse rounded out the cluster of buildings in the farmyard.

Rising behind the farm was a pretty, green hillside, steep enough to be a hard climb for Elisabeth's little legs. In Elisabeth's mind, the path up the hill was like a ladder, leading to different levels like the stories of a house. On the first story was the plum orchard, where Mother got the blue plums that dotted the top of Elisabeth's favorite *kuchen*. Walnut trees on the second story supplied nuts for a special treat: dainty cookies called *kleine küsse*,[8] "little kisses." On the third story grapevines flourished in the vineyard. Beyond the vineyard, on the fourth story, was a small house that held the winepress and other equipment for Father's winemaking. A sturdy wooden door led through the back wall of the house into the wine cellar, dug deep into the hill's clay soil. On the fifth story, at the top of the hill, the wheat field rustled in the breeze.

It was a beautiful place, that farm. Elisabeth loved her home, but not until she was forced to leave it did she realize how very dear it was to her.

Life on the farm was not always easy, of course. Elisabeth had her share of chores. By the time she was twelve, she fed the chickens, cleaned stalls, and worked in the fields—all by hand. It was hard work, yes, but not drudgery. Elisabeth was a vital part of the farm, and she knew it. Her work was important to the whole family. It needed to be done, and there was satisfaction in it.

Morning on the Winecker farm began with a picturesque routine still continued in Szárazd more than fifty years later. A visitor standing beside the street in the slanting morning light can watch the scene unfold just as Elisabeth might have so long ago:

*Along the quiet road comes a man carrying a long, flexible whip. Swinging it over his head, he cracks it with a noise like a shot. From the white farmhouse behind us a*

---

[8] klīn'-ə kuis'-ə; "uï" pronounced halfway between "oo" and "ih."
Mother's recipe for *kleine küsse* can be found on page 208.

*farmer appears, summoned by the sound of the whip. He enters the barn, unties each waiting cow and then returns to whatever business he has on hand. The animals, with an ease born of long habit, plod expectantly out of their stalls, down the path and onto the street, where they join their fellows emerging from barns all over Szárazd. The whip-wielder walks leisurely behind the growing herd as the cows make their way down the street and out of town, where they spend the day grazing in the open fields. In the same way the gate is opened for the sheep, and the flock gathers around the shepherd to be led out to the pastures. Even the pigs are turned loose; they too obediently follow their guardian outside the village to root around until evening.*

*As the sun lowers, the herds return. Moving slowly up the street, the animals automatically turn off, each at their own farm. The cows amble back to their stalls and wait to be*

*The cows plod their well-trained way home on a Szárazd afternoon.*

*tied up for the night. The sheep cluster into the fold, and the pigs run grunting back to the sty. When the last of the dwindling herd leaves the road, the man with the whip turns homeward, and in a few hours the village lies quietly sleeping, waiting for the crack of the whip to announce the start of another day.*

Elisabeth had her part in the daily routine as well. The young pigs went out with their mothers in the morning, but in the evening they were too slow to keep up with the rest of the herd. The owners were responsible to see they got safely back again. Whenever a sow on the Winecker farm had a litter of piglets, it was Elisabeth's job to go out to the pasture and bring them home. Elisabeth did not look forward to those walks. She was not terribly fond of animals, and anything out of the ordinary made her nervous, including venturing outside the village alone. There was no getting around any job Father gave her, so Elisabeth found a characteristic way to turn the trip into a pleasure: she persuaded her friends to come with her. The path over the gentle hills was beautiful, rich with the heady scent of blooming *acacia*[9] trees, and the company of friends made all the difference. The timid farm girl never imagined that in a few years she would walk alone through streets far more menacing than the quiet paths of Szárazd. That lay unseen in the future, and Elisabeth's childhood was a very happy one. Her fear of the unknown was balanced by a zest for life and a keen appreciation for fun.

---

9   a-kah'-see-ah; called black locust in the United States.

*On the stack of wheat shocks at harvest time, taken during the war.
From left to right: a refugee boy from Hamburg; Jakob and his wife,
Elisabeth's cousin Katharina; Elisabeth; Heini; Alfred (also from
Hamburg); Father, and a third boy from Hamburg.*

Farm life was busy and exciting, especially
during harvest time. Wheat harvest began in July.
Father mowed by hand, cutting the wheat with wide
sweeps of his sickle. Elisabeth followed him, laying
down sturdy cords of twisted straw that Father
wound during the winter. Behind her, Mother
gathered the severed wheat stalks into heaps on top
of the cords. Father re-crossed the field, mowing a
second swath, and Mother added the new stalks to
the growing mounds. When each mound was large
enough, Father jerked the string tight around it,
bound it securely and propped it upright. It was
hard, backbreaking work, but when it was finished

the jaunty shocks stood proudly erect, safe from rain and ready to take home for threshing.

The coming of the threshing machine was a long-remembered occasion. The big, steam-driven thresher traveled from farm to farm in harvest time. Elisabeth didn't know whose it really was—it was enough that it came! The greedy machine gobbled up the wheat stalks, and in an incredibly short time the wispy straw shot out one opening and the ripe, full grains poured out another.

Fascinating as the thresher was to watch, it was an unintended function of the machine that especially delighted the children. They stood in a line, holding hands expectantly, while the last child reached out and quickly touched a certain spot they had discovered on the thresher. With a zap, an electric

*A threshing machine similar to the one used in Elisabeth's village.*

shock ran through the line, causing great glee among the youngsters.

Not all the wheat was run through the rattling, steam-powered thresher; some was kept back and threshed by hand with long, wooden flails. The wheat was laid in two lines with the ears facing each other, and the kernels were beaten out with a rhythmic pounding of the swinging bars. *Pum, pum, pum, pum*—Elisabeth loved the sing-song sound of the flails, and the smooth, practiced motion that sent the heavy rod swinging on its leather hinge. In the winter, Father would twine the long straws from the hand-threshing into sheaf-strings for next year's wheat harvest.

Beside the rippling, golden wheat, there was another field that yielded a crop at least as useful, if not as familiar. This was *hanf*,[10] or hemp, a plant grown widely in Eastern Europe for its strong fibers. Twisted together and firmly plied, the *hanf* fibers made a sturdy rope. Coarsely spun, they were woven into practical aprons something like denim. Spun more finely and bleached in the sun, the *hanf* was transformed into beautiful tablecloths resembling fine linen. Soles for *paschke*,[11] the traditional knit shoes for indoor and outdoor wear; *nudeltuchen*,[12] cloths for drying the slender egg-noodles, and many other necessaries were made from the versatile *hanf*.

---

10 hahnf
11 pahsh'-kə
12 noo'-dle-too-kən

As Elisabeth grew, she learned the whole process of growing, harvesting, and processing *hanf*. The crop was an important one, and her father wanted to be certain she was well-prepared for the duties that would one day be hers as a farm wife.

When the *hanf* was ready for harvest, Elisabeth's first job was uprooting the mature plants. Since the Wineckers planted a large plot of *hanf*, and it had to be pulled up by hand, that was no small task. Each handful of stems was tied top and bottom with supple young *hanf* plants before being gathered into larger bundles and taken to the village pond. Here the bundles were placed in the water and left to ret, or soak, until the fibers softened.

Retrieving the *hanf* was the step Elisabeth dreaded. Wade into the pond's filthy, stagnant water? She refused to go into that water. Father was firm, despite her pleading and tears. If she was to take her part when she married, she must start now. Father's wisdom won the day, and Elisabeth, still crying, joined the ranks of the others working their *hanf* in the pond. The workers dredged up the slimy bundles, and then vigorously swung them in a circle over their heads, smacking them into the water each time to wash them.

The *hanf* was then dried and taken home for processing. The roots were cut off, and the stems beaten with a device called a scutcher to separate the fibers from the outer layers of stem. When Elisabeth was a baby, she had her own experience with the dried bits of stalks left by the scutcher. A neighbor boy, entrusted with babysitting Elisabeth, let the baby carriage run down the hill with her inside. The careening carriage tipped over, dumping Elisabeth into the pile of *hanf* chaff. The delinquent babysitter raced down the hill, picked up the screaming Elisabeth and dusted her off *schnell*[13] before a wrathful Oma Winecker could appear. Far from holding a grudge, Elisabeth remained good friends with her former babysitter long after they were both grown up.

After scutching, the *hanf* was carded with a round, nail-studded board, and then tied onto a distaff to keep the fibers from becoming tangled. Now the *hanf* was ready to be spun. The ladies of Szárazd gathered in the winter evenings to spin and visit, while the men laughed and talked. Mother left after dinner, and Father waited to put the children to bed before joining the men. Elisabeth and her brothers said their prayers with Father, and then lay quietly until he left the house. Once he was gone, they bounded out of bed to romp and play, laughing uproariously at their own jokes and antics. Seventy years later the memory of those evenings still set Elisabeth laughing.

On the Szárazd calendar, February 2 marked the end of the *hanf* spinning. By that date, all the fiber should be spun and ready to weave. Then Elisabeth's father sat at his loom, throwing the shuttle with smoothly swishing strokes as the cloth grew under his hand.

---

13 shnel; quickly, fast

*Hanf-scutching.*

The *hanf* cycle closely paralleled Elisabeth's own life, and no part was more applicable than Father's skillful weaving. As treadles and harnesses rose and fell under Father's measured judgment, so Elisabeth's childhood settled happily into the cyclical rhythms of Szárazd under the quiet direction of the Heavenly Father. As Father wound new strands of Mother's neatly spun *hanf* onto his shuttle, so God added threads of skill and knowledge to Elisabeth's tapestry as she grew; threads that would someday be more important than she could even guess. For now, like the little *hanf* plants, Elisabeth was growing straight and strong in her native field, relishing the changing phases of the farm year.

In October, the *mais*,[14] or corn on the cob, was ready for harvesting. Stripping the ears from the

---

14 mah-ees; the "ah" and "ee" run together into a single syllable.

stalks, the men dropped them into sacks as they moved down the rows of corn. The bags were emptied into a wagon bed, and when the wagon was full the cows pulled it home. That evening neighbors and friends gathered for the festive fun of a corn-shucking.

Throughout summer and fall, the garden provided a steady supply of vegetables under Oma Winecker's care. The onions for which Szárazd was locally famous, and which flourish only in the richest soils, grew in abundance. Mother braided the stems of onions and garlic into bunches to take to the market for sale. *Paprika,*[15] the Hungarian name for both sweet and hot peppers, added flavor to Oma's cooking. With a sturdy needle Elisabeth strung the hot peppers on a cord, then tied the ends together and hung the loop up to dry.

Then there was Father's vineyard, from which he made *riesling wein,*[16] the fine white wine sold to earn the much-needed yearly tax money. Father hung some of the grapes in the attic to sweeten until after the first frost, when the tiny orbs burst in the children's mouths with a sugary sweetness better than candy.

The bustling activity of the fall harvest was a vital time of preparation for the coming winter. Szárazd winters were snowy and severe. Mother knit thick black stockings to keep the children warm. Warm they were, but little Heini didn't appreciate

---

15 pah'-pree-kah
16 rees'-ling vine

the prickly wool. *"Ist kratzig,*[17] *ist kratzig,"* "It's scratchy, it's scratchy," he cried when he had to put them on. The freezing weather could be dangerous, though, and he had to wear them, itchy or not.

Elisabeth shoveled paths through the snowdrifts in the farmyard to keep up with the chores. One path was for her to reach the barn, another for the cows to reach their water trough. Another led to the woodshed, and others to the sheep barn and other outbuildings.

Winter was a time for indoor work, too. Weaving, spinning, sewing, knitting...all the jobs that were crowded out during the other three seasons by the work outside. Now was the time for repairing farm equipment and winding wheat-sheaf cords. If a wedding was expected, the ladies of Szárazd occupied the long evenings with another pastime. Every bride needed a plump, feather-filled comforter, and as the ladies sat cozily chatting they stripped the stiff shafts out of goose feathers, leaving only the soft vanes. Elisabeth still treasures the comforter the village ladies made for her mother.

As the long months of winter drew to a close, the village children began watching for the return of the swallows. One of the first harbingers of spring, the barn swallows arrived punctually every year from their winter quarters in southern Africa. Elisabeth loved to watch the glossy blue birds flit back and forth as they built their clustering nests in the barn and under the eaves. The zealous swallows were the

---

17 ist kraht'-seekh

farmers' friends. They rid the village of hated insect pests while catching tidbits to drop in the wide-open beaks of their little ones.

The return of the swallows marked the beginning of the new farm year. The winter wheat, lying dormant under the snow, would soon blanket the field with pricks of green. Planting season was at hand. Newborn lambs and large-eyed calves would soon join their mothers in the pilgrimage to the pastures. God's promise of uninterrupted seasons held good. The miracle of spring, of new life blossoming and growing, was about to begin again.

Life was good on the Winecker farm. Family and friends working together, vegetables fresh from the garden and fruit fresh from the trees, smoked sausages and meats from the smokehouse, fresh milk and bread...yes, it was a good, satisfying life, and fond memories of the farm's simple joys would shine in Elisabeth's mind through the troubled times to come.

# 3

## The Seedling's Field

*"He maketh me to lie down in green pastures: He leadeth me beside the still waters."*

~Psalm 23:2

Surrounding the garden plot of Elisabeth's own farm was the larger "field" in which she was growing. To reach that field, a traveler on Europe's great water highway, the Danube, journeys west from Austria along Hungary's northern border, and then turns south to follow the river into the heart of the land of the Magyars. Passing through the *Hauptstadt,*[1] magnificent Budapest, he continues southward into the fertile Tolna region of south-central Hungary. Here, below the important city of Paks,[2] the traveler leaves the Danube for the Sió[3] River. Journeying west and north, he winds through the ancient Szekszárd[4] vineyards, cultivated for over two thousand years. When the flat valley farmland gave

---

1   haupt'-shtadt; capital city
2   pahksh
3   shee-oh'
4   sek'-zard

Quelle: Deutsche Fotothek

*A white stork keeps watch over its brood.*

way to the rolling Kapos-Koppány[5] hills, he makes one final turn back to the southwest. A day's walk along the quiet Kapos River brings the traveler to Elisabeth's field: the village of Szárazd.

Szárazd lies in the mouth of a small valley at the edge of a wide swath of farmland. If the traveler arrives in May, swallows are already swooping overhead. Beneath the graceful swallows, bees bustle around the fragrant drooping clusters of the *acacia* trees. The bees ferry the nectar home to make clear, sweet acacia honey, the most prized honey in Europe. In the village proper, large, round stork nests adorn the chimneys. Each spring the tall white birds sail into Szárazd and stand guard on the

---

5   kah'-pōsh-koh-pah'-ny

rooftops as they raise their young. Neat, white farmhouses line the packed-earth roads, and the church steeple presides graciously over the scene.

The village of Szárazd was officially founded in 1737, though it had been sporadically inhabited for half a millennium. The ancient Celts built a settlement in the valley, and Serbs and Croats intermittently occupied the village before the invading Ottomans destroyed it in the 16th century. After the liberation of Hungary, the Austrian emperor granted the lands around Szárazd to Serbian officer Jossip Monasterly[6] as a reward for his services against the Turks. Monasterly needed industrious workers to improve the land, so he invited German settlers to the area. The prospect of working their own land attracted many, including peasants weary of the bondage of serfdom. The serfs, of course, were not free to leave, but some found ways to escape. "*Bei Nacht und Nebel*," in the night and in the fog, they slipped away to find a new life in Hungary.

Among the earliest families to settle in Szárazd were the Bechts, Elisabeth's mother's family. The family was originally from the disputed territory of Alsace,[7] whose strategic location on the Rhine River between France and Germany caused it to be conquered and reconquered by competing empires since Roman times. The Bechts were staunch Protestants, and during the Thirty Years' War the family fled to Germany to escape

6   yoh'-seep moh-nast'-ter-ly
7   ahl-sahss'

Catholic persecution. They were living in the region of Hesse when they heard and responded to Monasterly's invitation.

The rest of the Germans who settled in Szárazd were Protestants as well. The Lutheran immigrants faced stern resistance to their faith from the Catholic population outside their valley. A delegation of men from Szárazd, including Elisabeth's grandfather Becht, traveled all the way to the imperial court of Austria-Hungary in Vienna for permission to found a Lutheran Church in Szárazd. The emperor granted their petition, and the small community was allowed to worship in peace.

The little world of Szárazd was well-ordered and quiet. The villagers were hard-working, organized, and self-governing in the strictest sense. Their town was a model of neatness and productivity. Rich traditions governed nearly every aspect of life, and a departure from the time-honored customs was rare. A refusal to follow tradition was viewed as a rejection of the whole system of village life. The offender faced ostracism from the close ties that bound the villagers together.

Szárazd society centered around the Lutheran Church. The church building was two doors down from the Wineckers' house, and all Szárazd attended Sunday services in the picturesque chapel.

In the tower beneath the graceful steeple hung three church bells. These had their own part to play in the orderly round of Szárazd life. On Sunday mornings, one bell rang to call the villagers to church. When the service was about to begin, all three rang in a more insistent summons. Each evening the bells chimed to tell the children it was time to be home for the night, and woe betide the child who disregarded their call! It was so much fun to play outside, though, that Elisabeth and her friends often forgot to heed the bells' warning. Elisabeth had to learn her lesson many times from Father before she remembered to come home on time. Father's strict discipline was not pleasant, but later Elisabeth was thankful for his diligent training.

A single church bell also rang to bid farewell to those who departed Szárazd for their "long home."[8] A village funeral was a solemn and respectful time. The body was laid in a coffin in the family home while relatives, friends, and neighbors gathered to pay their last respects. For the funeral, the coffin was carried outside. The lid was closed after the service, and the coffin was lifted onto the pallbearers' shoulders. The church bell tolled slowly as the funeral procession wound its way through the town, and the solemn sound continued as the coffin was borne up the hill to the cemetery. When the mourners reached the gravesite, a white handkerchief was waved from the hill to signal the bell-ringer to halt, and the coffin was laid to rest in Szárazd's clay soil.

Elisabeth remembers two funerals particularly well. When she was eight years old, her great-grandmother Winecker passed away. Elisabeth

---

8  Ecclesiastes 12:5-7

looked into the coffin as it lay in the good room
before the funeral. It was the first time she had seen
a dead person. Father and Mother kindly explained
to her that Oma was gone to heaven. Elisabeth does
not remember being afraid, only sad that Oma had
gone away. At the funeral outside, Elisabeth saw the
neighbors' little girl standing in the yard next door.
Childlike, she remembers being quite proud that she
was allowed to attend the funeral, while her little
friend was not. The second funeral, not long after,
was memorable for a similar reason. Elisabeth and
her cousin, also named Elisabeth, stood together in
the crowd on the hillside. When they heard the new
widow sobbing beside the grave, the cousins thought
they were supposed to cry, too. They promptly
began to wail as loudly as they could, until Mother
quickly and quietly relieved them of their misplaced
sense of duty.

In Szárazd, relatives wore black mourning
dress for one year after the death of a family
member. Because extended families were large and
the infant mortality rate was high, some girls passed
their entire childhood in the somber black garb.
When not in mourning, the women and girls of
Szárazd wore the brightly-colored traditional
costumes of the village. All the dresses were similar
in style, but the free play of each woman's taste
resulted in a kaleidoscope of colors and textures.
Voluminous skirts, sometimes finely pleated, came
in a wide array of floral prints and colors. Starched
petticoats held out the yards of fabric, and

*A beautiful sampling of Szárazd dresses. This is one of Elisabeth's favorite pictures; everyone in it was her friend.*

decorative aprons covered the skirt in front. Elaborate borders on a lady's apron displayed her skill in lace-making and embroidery, and each had a different design to suit the wearer's fancy. The colorful jackets' square yokes and long sleeves boasted a multitude of trimmings and variations. Fastened closely around the high collars was a many-stranded necklace with a row of pointed beadwork on the lowest strand. Long-fringed black shawls were ringed with vivid, glowing flowers, and headscarves were tied under the chin in a manner distinctive to the region. Young girls wore similar costumes in miniature, with their hair plaited in two braids and crossed over their heads. When a girl married, she tied a *netzhaup,*[9] a round netted lace covering beaded with pearls, over the back of her head to cover her crossed braids. The pretty *netzhaup* distinguished the married *frau*[10] from the unmarried *fräulein.*[11]

At twelve years old, each child in the Lutheran church passed through the Lutheran confirmation ceremony. Intensive study of the Bible and church doctrine preceded the day itself, and the ritual was an important milestone in the lives of Szárazd's children. The girls wore special black dresses for the occasion, and after the ceremony each child was given a Bible verse. Elisabeth received Revelation 2:10.*"Be thou faithful unto death, and I will give thee a crown of life."*

Curiously, Elisabeth's father and mother, though confirmed several years apart, both received Psalm 37:5. *"Commit thy way unto the Lord; trust also in Him, and He shall bring it to pass."*

The verse given to her parents would come to have unique significance for Elisabeth. Again and again, in times of great strain and distress, Elisabeth watched the Lord honor that promise as she trusted Him.

*"Commit thy way unto the Lord; trust also in Him, and He shall bring it to pass."* Elisabeth was to choose those words as the guiding verse of her life, and her trust was never disappointed.

---

9   nets'-howp
10  frow
11  froi'-line

While the villagers steadfastly adhered to the outward forms of religion, over time they lost the living faith of their forefathers. By the turn of the twentieth century, membership in the Lutheran church and conformance to its customs were considered all the religious duty required to ensure entrance into heaven.

One day an itinerant barber entered the village. As he plied his trade from house to house, he shared a simple message with his customers; a message that shook the comfortable religious world of Szárazd to its foundations. He spoke of a relationship with Jesus, of a personal decision to accept the Savior's payment for sins and to follow Him as Lord. Some who listened believed, and a new life full of inner joy and peace began for them. It was not an easy life, however. The Lutheran church strongly condemned these new ideas, and the believers were forced to worship separately, meeting from house to house like the early Christians in the New Testament.

Despite the official church's disapproval and the scorn in which the "new believers" were held, more and more villagers began joining them. The persecution became more severe. Egg-throwing and name-calling became common in the streets of Szárazd, and petroleum was poured down the believers' wells. One wealthy family disowned their son and threw him out on the street when he embraced the new teachings. The maelstrom of anger and revenge that rocked the close-knit

community failed to shake the work God had begun
in Szárazd. The believers stood firm in their new-
found faith. Their steadfastness and loving example
were eventually rewarded by the salvation of many of
their former persecutors.

Elisabeth's family held aloof from both the
revival and the persecution that swept the village.
Father was an honorable, upright man, a good
husband and father, and he saw no need for any
change of heart. He respected the believers,
however, and while the Winecker family continued
to attend the Lutheran church on Sunday mornings,
on Sunday afternoons Father sent the children to the
believers' Sunday school.

Down the street from the Wineckers' house,
just past the church and the pastor's home, was the
schoolhouse. The school was Lutheran, like the
church, and the children memorized and studied the
Bible along with their standard academic subjects.
The structured classroom reinforced the habits of
obedience and respect that were hallmarks of
Szárazd's homes.

The school day began with a recited prayer:

*"Im Gottes Namen fang ich an,*
*was mir zu tun gebühret;*
*mit Gott wird alles wohlgetan*
*und glücklich ausgeführet.*
*Was man in Gottes Namen tut,*
*is allenthalben recht und gut*
*und kann uns auch gedeihen. Amen."*

*The class of the two-room Szárazd school. Elisabeth is seated third from right in the second row.*

"In God's name I begin to do
What is my duty meted;
When done with God, all is done well,
And happily completed.
What in God's name we do with grace,
Is right and good in every place,
And can our doings prosper. Amen."

The schoolhouse was divided into two rooms; the first through fourth grades met in one, and the fifth through eighth in the other. As in early American schools, the children studied their lessons at home and recited them from memory in the classroom.

Due to the nationalistic movement for "Magyarization" in Hungary, lessons were primarily in Hungarian, which was very difficult at first for the

German-speaking children. Elisabeth memorized and recited entire history lessons in Hungarian, but she hardly understood a word she said. Foreign language students can appreciate the task she faced; memorizing in one's own language is difficult enough, but remembering long passages of meaningless sounds is far harder. The feat speaks volumes for the quickness of Elisabeth's mind. Once she had to learn and recite a Hungarian poem, and she learned it well. Decades later she could still declaim the stirring words with gusto, but had no idea what they meant.

Each child owned a slate, blank on one side for arithmetic exercises and lined on the other for handwriting practice. Most of the children's writing classes were in Hungarian, but they were taught a bit of German writing as well. Elisabeth's little hands struggled with the Old German cursive script. She has a vivid memory of one of their German writing assignments. For some reason, the picture of a little girl standing on a chair and reaching up for a container of sugar stayed in her mind, and so did the caption that formed the basis for their composition: *"Der Kaffee ist nicht süß genug,"* "The Coffee is not Sweet Enough."

Like her father, Elisabeth was an apt student. Almost unbroken columns of *kitűnő* and *jeles* run down the pages of her little school record book, and she was consistently commended for her behavior and

*Elisabeth's record book, showing her grades for the 1939-1940 school year.*

diligence. She received particularly outstanding grades for *Ének,*[12] singing, which she dearly loved.

Elisabeth enjoyed school. Like the work at home, it needed to be done, and to her it was fun. She studied well and was rarely in disgrace, but she clearly remembers the day that no one in her class of ten girls and four boys could remember the Hungarian name for England. They looked at each other in dismay. There was no help for it; none of them knew. After seventy years Elisabeth still remembered the sentence the teacher made them write one hundred times each as punishment: *"Brit-*

---

12 ay'-nək

*sziget Angol órszag."* "The British island is *England."*
Father wasn't too pleased when he heard she had
been punished, either!

At noon the students were dismissed for
dinner. Even in harvest time the villagers stopped
their work and took time to eat at home together.
Except on rare occasions when work was being done
in a far-off field, the entire Winecker family gathered
around the table for the main meal of the day.

When the Winecker children were small, they
learned a short prayer to say before the meal:

> *"Alle guten Gaben,*
> *Alles was wir haben,*
> *Kommt o Gott von dir.*
> *Dank sei dir dafür.*
> *Amen."*

> "Every good gift given,
> Everything we have,
> Comes, oh God, from Thee,
> And so we thank Thee.
> Amen."

And when they were a bit older, they learned
the prayer that Elisabeth still liked to say before
meals when she was over eighty years old:

> *"Komm, Herr Jesus, sei unser Gast,*
> *Und segne, was Du uns aus Gnaden bescheret hast.*
> *Amen."*

"Come, Lord Jesus, be our Guest,
And may these gifts of grace from You be blest.
Amen."

Father taught Elisabeth and her brothers to
eat everything on their plates, whether they liked it
or not.

"I don't like everything in the same way
either," Father told them, "but that was cooked with
love, and you need to eat it."

Oma's hearty dinners were calculated to give
strength for the hard farm labor. As in many German
houses today, every dinner began with soup. In
summer, the broth was filled with whatever
vegetables Oma picked in the garden that day. In
winter, the pot was thick with beans or potatoes. A
plate of *wurst*[13] or other meat was usually on the
table, along with Mother's fresh bread and a ceramic
pitcher of cold well-water.

After dinner the children returned to school
for the afternoon. When their studies for the day
were over, they rose and repeated the closing prayer:

*"Aus der Schule geh ich fort,*
*Herr bleib bei uns mit deinen Wort;*
*Mit deiner Gnade und Segen*
*Auf allen unseren wegen.*
*Amen."*

---

13 verst; there are over a thousand varieties of these beloved,
distinctively German sausages.

"As from the school I now go forth,
Lord, let Thy Word beside us stay;
And send Thy grace and blessing here
To walk with us on all our way.
Amen."

In keeping with the order so characteristic of Szárazd, the students formed two neat lines and marched respectfully out of the schoolhouse. Once outside the door, they scattered cheerfully to their homes or to play.

The evening meal was cold, often bread with homemade cheese and sausage, and afterward the children turned to their studies. Mother helped Elisabeth memorize her lessons, and then Father quizzed her on them.

On Saturday nights, the family made special preparations for Sunday. Mother sewed new *hanf* soles on the children's *paschke,* using multi-sized wooden lasts, or shoe forms, carved by Opa Becht. Father gave the children their baths in a stall set aside for the purpose, and the family made ready for the call of the church bells to celebrate the Lord's Day in the morning.

Along with the church bells, Szárazd had a prescribed, orderly method of spreading information. When an official announcement or important piece of news needed to reach the village, the drummer was sent out from the town hall. Every two or three houses he halted, beating his drum to call the

inhabitants out to the street. Once they gathered, he
roundly delivered his message. When finished, he
walked a few houses farther and struck up his
drum again. The rolling drumbeats sounded around
the village until every home in Szárazd had heard
the news.

There was one faction of Szárazd society that
was not as orderly as the rest. These were the
Gypsies. They lived close by, but not in the village,
and occasionally they drove their horse-drawn
wagons into Szárazd. One wagon Elisabeth
remembered particularly well: the one that sold
watermelons! Sometimes Father or Mother would
buy one, sometimes not, but Elisabeth's hopes made
that wagon her favorite. The Gypsies went from
house to house, offering to sharpen scissors or buy
any cast-off clothes or household wares. When a pig
was slaughtered, the Gypsies asked for the bones,
and if a chicken was old—or even if one died—they
asked for that as well.

It was a different life, that roving, Gypsy life,
and children the world over tend to mock anything
"different." The village children of Szárazd were no
exception. One day Elisabeth and her little friends
followed the Gypsies out to their camp, singing
teasing, scornful words as they went. Their brashness
was tempered with caution; they sang in Hungarian,
which they knew the Gypsies did not understand.
The excursion would not have been so memorable
except that the children had an unexpected listener.
Father heard them. Elisabeth's unkindness received

its due punishment, and Father made it clear in no uncertain terms that teasing others simply for being Gypsies, which they could not help, was not acceptable. Elisabeth never found out if her friends experienced similar consequences, but she, at least, never forgot that lesson.

The children of Szárazd were a happy lot, and their exuberant play changed with the changing seasons. In the rainy spring, when runoff from the hills turned the streets into miniature rivers, the children gathered to frolic in barefooted delight in the muddy water. In summer, they picked tiny, fragrant linden flowers to dry for tea, or climbed the neighbors' mulberry tree to munch on dark purple berries before jumping down again. In the frigid winter, sleds ran riot over the snowy hills.

Summer vacation gave extra time for play, and the children organized a "store" with one child as the proprietor. The other children gathered their spending money from the trees. The store accepted a currency of small round *acacia* leaflets. The smallest leaflets, picked from the tips of the long compound leaves, became one-*fillér*[14] coins; the larger leaflets farther up were worth two *fillér*, and so on.

Another exciting season for the children arrived in December, when they prepared and performed a Christmas program for the village. The children memorized the Christmas portions of the Gospels and took turns reciting the beautiful story of

---

14 Pronounced halfway between fill-eer' and fill-air', the fillér was the Hungarian equivalent of the American penny;

the Savior's birth. Every child offered a verse, poem, or song as their contribution to the festivities.

Music and poetry pervaded Szárazd tradition. There was a poem or song for almost everything, from the bridegroom's eloquent summons for his bride to the child's carefree swinging on a swing. On no other day, perhaps, did the children recite their well-learned verses with more relish than on the

*The three Winecker children. Left to right: Hans, Elisabeth, Heini. Hans and Heini are wearing* paschke, *traditional knit shoes.*

joyously celebrated New Year's morning. Carrying
little drawstring bags and well-bundled against the
cold, the little forms trudged excitedly from house to
house. As doors opened to reveal friends, neighbors,
and relatives, each child recited a poem bringing
New Year's blessings and prayers to the household.
In appreciation, a ten-*fillér* piece or other small coin
was dropped into each outstretched bag. From Opa
Becht Elisabeth might even get a *pengő*, a Hungarian
dollar.[15] Older children's poems were long and
sometimes beautifully worded, such as this one
Elisabeth remembers reciting:

> *"Ein neues Jahr, ein neues Leben,*
> *fängt Heut an diesem Morgen an.*
> *Wir Danken Gott ders uns gegeben,*
> *und unser Lob steigt Himmel an.*
>
> *Das alte Jahr ist nun verflossen,*
> *bei mancher Not und Traurigkeit.*
> *Doch uns hat Gottes Lieb umschlossen*
> *und nur geschützt vor allem Leid.*
>
> *Das neue Jahr bringt uns nur Segen;*
> *Gesundheit, Glück, und Wohlergehen,*
> *Not Krankheit mög uns nie umstehen,*

---

15 The Hungarian *pengő* (pang'-uh) was introduced in 1927 to replace
   the former unit of currency, the *korona*. In the economic chaos
   following World War II, the worst rate of hyperinflation in history
   caused the *pengő* to be replaced in August of 1946 by the *forint,* at
   the rate of 400,000,000,000,000,000,000,000,000,000 (400,000
   quadrillion) to 1.

*erhöre Gott unser kindlich Flehen.*
*Amen."*

"A brand new year, a brand new life,
This morn to us is given.
With thanks to God for this new gift,
Our praises rise to heaven.

The former year has passed away,
With hardship and with sadness;
From suffering we have been spared,
Held in God's love with gladness.

The new year only blessing brings;
Health, happiness, well-being.
Oh God, protect from all distress,
And hear our childlike pleading.
Amen."

This whimsical verse for the little ones was
simple and to the point:

*"Wünsche, wünsche, weiß nicht was,*
*Greifen Sack und gib mir was!"*

"I wish, I wish, I don't know what;
Reach in your bag and give me something!"

As Elisabeth grew a bit older, she joined the
young people who congregated on winter nights as
the adults did. The girls clustered around a single

hanging lamp to knit, while the young men gathered talking around a nearby table. They were a fun-loving group, and Elisabeth took her full part in the laughter and fun around her. One of the young men at the table began to show marked interest in the bright-eyed girl under the lamp. It wouldn't be long before he began escorting Elisabeth home from the winter gatherings. On some evenings knitting was laid aside, and the faint sounds of singing, music, and dancing filtered through the warmly shuttered windows into the cold air outside.

Elisabeth's field...she and many others loved that little village with undying affection. In the turbulent days to come, the peaceful village life seemed like an idyllic vision, a dream-existence. The dream followed those who had lived there for the rest of their lives. To them and to Elisabeth, no other earthly place would ever be so dear as that beloved valley. In their hearts, Szárazd would always be *home.*

# 4

## A Lurking Storm

*"All these are the beginning of sorrows."*
*~Matthew 24:8*

The Weaver was about to interrupt the quiet pattern on Elisabeth's tapestry, and not on hers only, but on the fabric of world history as well. The Hand holding the shuttle did not fumble or slip, but began to allow threads that, to human eyes, seemed unthinkably dark and confused. A time of great darkness was approaching, when the glory of God's goodness would shine with increasing brightness against the blackness of evil created by men.

Elisabeth, less than twelve years old, understood little of the political turmoil swirling around her country in the late thirties. Hungary was caught between two great political forces, Germany and Russia, as they competed for control of Eastern Europe. In an effort to win Hungary to its side, Germany played skillfully on the smoldering resentment left from the aftermath of World War I. Under protest, defeated Hungary had been compelled to sign the 1920 Treaty of Trianon, which

*The result of the struggle is illustrated by another look into Elisabeth's little school record book. In the years 1937, '38, and '39, the report cards are acknowledged by her father's Hungarian signature: Winecker J'anos. In the school year of 1940-'41, when Elisabeth was twelve years old, the Hungarian is abruptly replaced by the conquering German, and Father's name is written in Germanic style as "Johann Winecker."*

stripped the country of nearly three-fourths of its territory and of its only seaport. In 1938 and 1940, Germany and Italy issued the Vienna Awards, forcing Czechoslovakia and Romania to return some of the forfeited territories to the Hungarian Crown. The Reich's political maneuvering was successful. On November 20, 1940, Hungary signed the Tripartite Pact and allied itself with the Axis powers.

At first, the new alliance mattered little to the villagers of Szárazd. They, like the unsuspecting inhabitants of Laish,[1] dwelt "quiet and secure," far from troubling matters of state and the threat of national war. Their well-loved routine remained largely undisturbed. Farming continued as usual, as did school, though lessons were now primarily in German.

The shadow of war hardly shaded the sun as it shone down on a new but age-old season beginning for Elisabeth. In Szárazd, girls usually married between fifteen and seventeen years of age. At eighteen or nineteen, a girl was old! And as Elisabeth approached her teenage years, marriage was not just a distant possibility. The young man who walked her home from the winter gatherings had made his preference for her well known. Heinrich Frank[2] was a few years older than Elisabeth, the only son in his family, and was well-liked by all of Szárazd. He was also Father's choice of all the young men in the village; a fine indication of his character. Though Elisabeth returned Heinrich's admiration, she was still too young to know how to give him more than the warm friendship she gave all her comrades.

Gradually, effects of the titanic struggle convulsing the world rippled into the isolated village. A new group for young people, the "*Hitler Jugend,*"[3] or Hitler Youth, was formed, and the children of Szárazd were invited to join. The villagers knew very little about Hitler. They heard that he was a good

---

1   Judges 18:7
2   hīn'-rik frahnk
3   yoo'-gənd

man—he helped the poor and built the Autobahn—
but beyond that their ignorance was almost
complete. Of his political agenda and philosophies
they knew nothing. To them, he was an able leader
who had accomplished much for Germany and her
people, and this brought him credit in their eyes.
The villagers had clung to their German ancestry
despite Hungary's Magyarization programs, and were
relieved and happy to see the growing German
influence in Hungary.

German recruiters came to the village with
glowing tales of what the glorious Reich had to offer.
They promised Heinrich Frank a university
education. Another young man, tall, blond, and
athletic, was assured training as an Olympic
runner. The young villagers, faced with
opportunities they had only dreamed of, were too
naïve to suspect treachery.

Heinrich said good-bye to Elisabeth and set
off, as he thought, for the university. Instead, he was
given nothing but a rifle and sent to the front lines.
Those who didn't volunteer were soon drafted; most
of them, like Heinrich, into the Waffen SS. One
entire family—a father and two sons—received draft
notices. They locked the door behind them and left
their farmhouse empty. Every young man in Szárazd
was swallowed up by the insatiable German war
machine, and horrifyingly few ever returned.

A Jewish family living in Szárazd also
disappeared. The Germans said the family had been
moved somewhere to work, and the explanation

satisfied the villagers, who had no idea of the grisly web that had entangled their neighbors. As far as Elisabeth knows, the entire family died in the concentration camps, where work was a grim prelude to death.

The war grew still more tangible when a division of *Hitler Jugend* arrived in Szárazd with their leader, seeking refuge from the Allied bombing. The

*Heinrich Frank.*

Wineckers hosted two boys, one from bombed-out Hamburg,[4] and heard stories of the terrible effects of the air raids. The boys repeated a saying that translates to something like this: "The earth itself cannot hide you; anywhere you go the bombs will find you." Such fear was far removed from Elisabeth's peaceful valley.

In 1943, in the midst of the annual harvest-time bustle, Elisabeth began to feel ill. At first it was only a stomach-ache, and she thought she had eaten

*Heinrich Frank in German uniform.*

---

4　The boy from Hamburg, named Alfred, kept in contact with the Winecker family. Years after the war, Elisabeth traveled to Hamburg to visit him and his wife and children.

too many apricots. When she didn't get better, Father sent her inside to rest in the quiet of the good room. Elisabeth lay on the carefully-guarded green couch, staring at the red roses and feeling too awful to enjoy the rare privilege.

The pain grew so much worse that finally Mother sent for Opa Becht. He took them in his wagon to the hospital, 18 miles away, where the doctors discovered that Elisabeth had appendicitis. The enormous, crowded room where they waited for the surgery stands vividly in Elisabeth's memory. After the operation, she woke up in a small private room with only her mother and two friends. Two weary weeks crawled by in the hospital. Opa Becht bicycled all the way from Szárazd to visit, bringing much-needed laughter and fun.

Elisabeth returned home to finish her convalescence, and a few months later new joy came to the Winecker farm. The baby girl born on December 26, 1943, was a precious Christmas gift from God. Baby Katharina was named for Oma Winecker, and nicknamed Kathi.[5] After fourteen years as the only daughter in the family, Elisabeth had a little sister.

The new year brought change of a different kind. At thirteen, Elisabeth had been too young to understand Heinrich's feelings for her. At fifteen, she understood. His postcards were treasures to be read and re-read. In 1944, he returned briefly on leave. What must have been the sweetness of that

5  kah'-thee

reunion, and what joy for Heinrich to find that Elisabeth now fully shared his hopes for the future!

Heinrich's division was sent to the Eastern Front after his return, and on the first of September he mailed a postcard from Nagyvárad,[6] in far eastern Hungary. The brief note read, *"Greetings from my heart, from Nagyvárad. From your Heinrich Frank."*

Not long after the postcard arrived, a black thread shot through Elisabeth's tapestry. The entire town mourned when the news came that Heinrich Frank would not be coming home. Fatally wounded by the Russians, he joined the vanished ranks of those who "didn't come back."

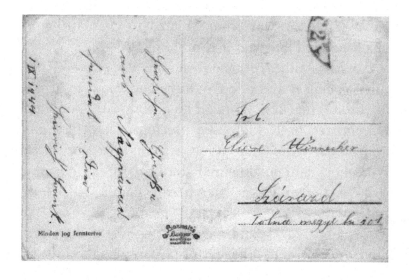

*(Above and on facing page) Heinrich chose a postcard with pull-out views of Nagyvárad's scenic landmarks to send to his sweetheart back in Szárazd.*

---

6   nadj-vah'-rad. Present-day Oradea, Romania.

In August, 1944, Father, too, was drafted. Leaving his family at that time must have been especially difficult. Mother, always in fragile health, had contracted tuberculosis. It was the middle of harvest season, and the burden of working the farm would fall on the three older children. Father knew from bitter experience what his children faced.

For Oma Winecker, too, memories must have made the separation a hard one. Thirty years before, she said good-bye to her husband as he set off to war, and that farewell had been forever. Now she was saying good-bye to her only son. The parting was ominously reminiscent of Opa Winecker's departure. Father's unit, too, was bound for Yugoslavia.

Elisabeth, Hans, and Heini took over the work of the farm. Father's training now began to prove its worth, but even though Elisabeth knew what needed to be done, getting in the harvest without Father and Mother's help was an enormous task.

Elisabeth remembers one incident that lightened that dark time. The three children were trying to sow the winter wheat. Elisabeth led the cows in front, Hans guided the seeder, and Heini walked behind to make sure the machine worked properly. The cows were not being cooperative. Elisabeth struggled unsuccessfully to make them pull a straight furrow. Finally Hans lost patience with her. He called authoritatively from the seeder, "You come back here!"

Surprised at the command from her eleven-year-old brother, Elisabeth obeyed. Hans sent little Heini up front, and Elisabeth watched in astonishment as the stubborn cows at once began pulling smoothly. The rest of the field was sown without any trouble. Elisabeth never had been very good with the cows!

There was not much else to smile about. In a few short months, the peaceful life of Szárazd was transformed into a world of darkness and fear. In October, the Russians launched the Budapest

*Father in German army uniform.*

Offensive. Rumors of Soviet advances became more and more threatening. With all but the elderly men gone, the women were painfully aware of their vulnerability should the Axis defense fail.

German bombers *en route* to Russian positions became increasingly common in Szárazd's formerly quiet skies. Hugging the ground to avoid detection, the planes flew so low that the watching villagers could see the pilots' faces. The bass roar of the throbbing engines shook the ground.

One day Elisabeth was working with a group of friends in the hayfield when another in the daily string of bombers approached. This time the passing string was broken. As the bomber roared past, an explosion rocked the valley. Elisabeth spun around to see an expanding cloud of smoke rising from the village. Her horrified eyes saw that it stood directly above her home—*her home*—and Mother had been in the house! Elisabeth started to rush home, but the other girls stopped her.

"My mother is there—my house is *kaput!*"[7] Elisabeth cried as her friends tried to calm her.

"We need to wait and go together," they said. "We don't know where it really hit."

They hurried back to the village in a group, and Elisabeth's relief was intense when they came in sight of the farmhouse, standing intact. The bomb struck just outside the edge of the village; it was only from the field that the smoke seemed to come from the Winecker farm.

---

7   kah-put', with "put" to rhyme with "foot;" broken, ruined.

After discussion, the villagers decided that the bomb had been dropped accidentally. In the Lord's grace, no one was injured, but the incident added to the rapidly-mounting stress on the villagers. The constant tension and fear were almost unbearable.

The relentless Soviet offensive continued. As the Red Army pushed closer, an agonizing decision confronted the women of Szárazd. Go, or stay? They had heard reports of the Russian soldiers' brutality, and the little village was almost completely undefended. But if they fled, what would become of their homes? And how would their men ever find them? The husbands and fathers of Szárazd had taken their responsibility as family leaders seriously, and borne the weight of all important decisions. Suddenly the women were faced with life-changing, possibly irreversible choices, without a chance to even ask their men.

For some, the Lord made the choice easier. Elisabeth's good friend Elisabeth Schell was one of these. When her father, Georg Schell, left for the army, he gave Elisabeth the responsibility of looking after the farm since her mother was unable to do so. Though terribly afraid of the Russians, Elisabeth was determined to stay and keep her promise to him. In the Lord's kindness, a letter from her father somehow found its way from Yugoslavia to Szárazd. Georg Schell had seen the horror of the Russian front, and told his daughter unequivocally to flee if she found an opportunity. Released from her promise, Elisabeth began packing. Her mother was

aghast at the thought of leaving her home. As quickly
as Elisabeth packed the bags, her mother unpacked
them. Elisabeth, however, had her father's
permission—nay, his command—and she was now as
determined to leave as she had been to stay.

The Wineckers, too, received a letter. How
the fragile envelope survived the journey from war-
torn Yugoslavia through the chaos engulfing Hungary
was a miracle of the Lord's love and care. Father, too,
had seen the vicious reality of the *Ostfront.*[8] He still
respected the Szárazd believers, and said that if the
believers found an opportunity to flee, the family
should go with them. Those words relieved Mother
of the burden of the decision. They would go. Now
it was only a question of *when.*

---

8    ahst'-front; literally, "Eastern Front," referring to the brutal line of
     Axis-Soviet conflict in Eastern Europe which cost more than 30
     million lives, both military and civilian.

# 5

## Uprooted

*"Thus the Lord preserved David
whithersoever he went."*
~ *I Chronicles 18:6*

In the dim light of an early Sunday morning,
November 26, 1944, Elisabeth and her mother were
roused from their beds by a sudden pounding at the
farmhouse door. Elisabeth's aunt cried through the
boards, "Are you still in bed? We're leaving today!"

Aunt Barbara quickly explained that the
German army had made an empty freight train
available, and the believers were seizing the
opportunity to escape. Hitler had requested the
temporary evacuation of all Germans within thirty
miles of the Danube River. A secret weapon, the
Führer announced, would then destroy the invading
Russians and the people would be allowed to return
in peace. Secret weapons were far beyond the realm
of Szárazd's knowledge, but the order gave the
believers the chance they had been waiting for. The
train was being held until the huge thresher could be
brought to the station, but there was no time to lose.

Leaving! The morning was quiet no longer. Mother began stuffing clothing and supplies into *hanf* sacks for the journey. The autumn weather was cold, and she had the children pull on extra layers of clothes.

"Go run to Opa's house," Mother told Elisabeth, "and ask him to drive us to the station."

Elisabeth pounded down the familiar road to her grandparents' home. To her surprise, when she repeated Mother's request, Opa refused.

"I can't do that," he said, his voice tired and sad. Opa didn't think they should go, and was unwilling to help them carry out what he considered a dangerous decision. His own decision to stay was influenced by the fact that he had more to lose than they did. His fine house, his many possessions, held him firmly. He couldn't bear to leave it all to be plundered. He was staying. Many of the other villagers stayed, too, preferring the chance of safety at home to the uncertainty of venturing into the unknown.

Elisabeth gave up and rushed home again. A horse-drawn wagon driven by Russian prisoners-of-war pulled up at the farmhouse, offering to carry goods to the station. Sacks of clothing and bedding, Mother's feather comforter, the little spinning wheels...one by one the familiar trappings of home were carried out and loaded into the wagon bed. But in the flurried rush, one treasure was forgotten. In an oversight Elisabeth regretted for the rest of her life, the huge family Bible was left behind.

Soon the last bundle was loaded. The family began climbing into the wagon for the ride to the station, less than a mile away. Elisabeth hung back.

"It's Sunday; I want to go to church," she begged her mother. That morning the Russian prisoners were singing after the service, and Elisabeth dearly wanted to hear them. She ran up the road, hurried up the stone steps, and slipped inside the church door. The service had already begun. When it ended, the congregation moved outside for the concert. The "White Russian" soldiers from Belarus could *sing*. Elisabeth stood entranced by the haunting harmonies of the Slavic songs. During a pause in the singing someone noticed the girl standing there.

"Winecker, are you still here?" they cried, knowing her family was leaving and horrified that she wasn't at the station. "You'd better go!"

Elisabeth obediently disappeared, but instead of heading for the train station she turned back to walk one last time through the silent farmhouse. The thought of never seeing those well-loved rooms again was overwhelming. Weeping, she wandered through the house, fixing each room in her memory. Finally, catching up a few little things she didn't want left behind, Elisabeth tore herself away. As she closed and locked the double door before running toward the station, she closed it not only on the home she loved, but on the happy, carefree childhood she would never know again.

The bustle at the train station was tremendous. Families hurriedly loaded their belongings into the empty boxcars. Sacks and goods were piled high against the bare walls, leaving only a small space on the floor for sitting and sleeping. The thresher was finally loaded onto a flat car, but delays took up the whole day and the following night. On Monday morning, November 27, the train was ready to leave.

Elisabeth Schell ran up at the last moment. After hearing that the Russians shot animals on sight, she shut her beloved dog in the barn, hoping to keep him safe. Somehow he managed to escape and follow her to the station. Elisabeth couldn't bear the thought of the Russians killing him, and though the train was about to leave she ran with him all the way back to the village. Shutting him securely in, she dashed back to the station just before the train pulled out.

As the train passed Szárazd, the families rolled back the boxcar doors and crowded around for a last look at home. As Elisabeth looked out, she saw friends running to the brow of the hill behind the church for a final good-bye. Waving and crying, they watched the train chug past, while those on board waved and cried in return. None of them knew what the future would bring, either for those going out into the strange unknown, or for those remaining in the fragile security of home. Little Heini laughed

*Ethnic German refugees board a train in Romania in a scene similar to that in Szárazd.*

and waved in delight. Too young to understand, he thought the whole adventure was great fun.

The train ride was not a comfortable one. The boxcars were designed for freight, not passengers, and were severely overcrowded. It was hard to find room for everyone to lie down at once, but they did the best they could. The cars had no windows, and the only source of fresh air came through small vents near the roof. The vents became portholes to the outside world, as the boys clambered up the walls to peer out at the passing landscape.

The physical discomfort added to the villagers' inner turmoil. Szárazd's sheltered valley, the only home they knew, was fading rapidly into the distance. All that was familiar faded with it, and none of them knew when—or if—they would be able to return. The sudden severing of so many ties was hard enough for the young people, but for the older generation, Elisabeth remembered, it was like death.

"How would that be for us today?" she asked. "Somebody comes, you close the door, and go. And you don't know where. You leave everything there. We were farmers; everything was there. That is hard to understand. What you saved, what you had for years...and just leave it there. That was so hard. I mean, we were children, but for the elderly people—they were just broken down."

The grief they left behind was magnified by the uncertainty ahead. The villagers had no idea where the train was taking them, or what life would be like when they climbed out of the closed-in boxcars. Their uneasiness grew when they heard rumors of spies on board the train. The travelers were closely questioned. Elisabeth and her family knew nothing of Hitler or of spies; the questions only confused them, and Szárazd began to seem very far away.

The wheels rumbled rhythmically along the tracks, carrying the refugees farther and farther to the northwest. Suddenly the train braked swiftly, and the familiar clatter was replaced by an unnerving silence. The tracks ahead were blocked by another train. A bomber had scored a direct hit, and the engine was *kaput*. With no way to move the crippled locomotive, both trains were stranded. There was nothing to do but wait.

Waiting became more than a simple annoyance when the families began running out of food. The tracks ran through the middle of the countryside with no place to buy supplies, so a small foraging party formed. The leader was Jakob,[1] Elisabeth's cousin Katharina's husband. Jakob's presence with the refugees was unusual. He had been drafted into the German army with the other men, but because of a sickness in the family he had been allowed to return home. He was still on leave when the believers fled, so he accompanied his family. Elisabeth, her friend Barbara, and Barbara's younger brother Hans formed the rest of the party.

The little group headed off, leaving the motionless train behind. They found a small village nearby where they were able to buy apples. Triumphantly they returned to the railroad, and as they reached the tracks Jakob swung his apples onto the train. As the sack hit the floor of the car, the train lurched forward and began to move. In a flash Jakob realized the train was leaving; the tracks must have been cleared while they were gone. With less than a moment to weigh the consequences, he made a desperate decision. He was a strong, active young man, and could easily swing himself onto the car and continue the journey with his family. But the three children couldn't. They would be left alone and unprotected, with little chance of ever seeing their families again. In that split second, Jakob chose to stay with them.

---

1   yah'-kəb

Together they stood by the tracks, staring after the disappearing train. An almost overpowering fear caught at Elisabeth. They had been left behind. Their families were gone. How would they ever find them?

The children would have been lost without Jakob's leadership and presence of mind. He led them along the tracks until they were overtaken by another train and allowed to board. Then began a long, weary, and seemingly hopeless chase. The rails were crowded with trains, all nearly alike, all filled to the brim with refugees. The children watched in vain for the threshing machine that marked the back of their train. There was no sign of the thresher, or of the familiar faces from Szárazd. Changing from train to train as they could, jumping from one and running to the next, the little group traveled on.

Two or three trains later, with the day almost gone, they reached an army post. The Germans were suspicious of Jakob's civilian dress and questioned him strictly. Why was he not with his unit? Jakob explained his leave of absence, and the unexpected circumstance that left him in charge of the children. The soldiers were not fully satisfied with his answers, but they were more than kind to the weary children. They welcomed them in, fed them, and gave them a place to lie down. Elisabeth and her friends were so exhausted that they slept despite their worry. They had hardly dozed off when the soldiers woke them again.

"Come!" the soldiers cried, "there's another train and you can go."

The children were hurried on board. The soldiers permitted Jakob to accompany them, and again the rumbling wheels carried them swiftly away.

Elisabeth's mind was as crowded as the endless boxcars. How could they find their train? How could they find their families? Elisabeth did not yet know God, but she had learned in church and school that He was powerful, and she knew that He could help her now.

*"Commit thy way unto the Lord,"* read her parents' confirmation verse. *"Trust also in Him, and He shall bring it to pass." (Psalm 37:5)*

In this sudden crisis, Elisabeth put her trust in the Lord. Desperately she prayed and depended on Him as the search continued.

Far up the line the train pulled to a stop in the teeming confusion of a major rail yard. Trains filled the rows of tracks, and the sea of humanity was bewildering. German soldiers distributed watery soup to the masses of refugees. It was rumored to be horse meat, but the children were so hungry that they ate it anyway. Suddenly, on a flat car at the back of one of the nondescript trains, they saw a huge, ungainly piece of machinery. The little group rushed forward. The threshing machine! That was the train from Szárazd!

The relief of that reunion was tremendous. The feelings of the two mothers as they watched their children left behind can be imagined. The separation had been a severe ordeal for them. Oma Winecker declared that from the time the train began to move until the moment they saw each other again she had not stopped praying. The family clustered around to offer a heartfelt *"Danke Herr²"* to the Lord who had done the impossible.

*"Trust also in Him, and He shall bring it to pass."* The words had proved true for the first of many times in Elisabeth's life. Even today she has no idea how the family found each other. Scores of families separated by the war were not reunited for years, if at all. The Master Weaver had firm hold on the threads, and His hand had been hard at work. The self-sacrificing guidance and protection He provided in Jakob were especially poignant. A short time later Jakob was recalled to the army, and never returned.

The Wineckers were intensely happy to be together as the train journey continued. Vienna, Queen of the Blue Danube, was their destination, but when they arrived the refugees were not allowed to enter. Like the train engine that caused so much trouble, Vienna, Elisabeth said, was *kaput.* Allied bombers pounded the city day and night, striking heavy blows at the critically important oil refinery and the industrial strength of the Axis.

Two powerful new locomotives were coupled to the train, and at breathtaking speed they plunged westward. The rails led on, across the Austrian border and over the Inn River just before its

---

2   dahn-kə hair; "Thank you, Lord."

confluence with the Danube. On the other side of the river lay the land where the refugees hoped to find safety: the German state of Bavaria.

# 6

## *Muddy Waters*

*"The Lord maketh poor, and maketh rich:
He bringeth low, and lifteth up."*

~*I Samuel 2:7*

Germany. How little the refugees knew of the
dark secrets harbored by that land when they arrived
there seeking Hitler's protection. Not until the war
was over would they and many other Germans learn
of the Nazis' underground chain of horror. That
horror was still hidden in 1944, when the train
carrying the Szárazd refugees crossed the border into
the villagers' ancestral homeland.

The train rumbled through Passau, the "City
of Three Rivers," where the converging waters of the
Ilz and Inn swell the Danube's mighty stream. On
into the Bavarian countryside, the tracks followed
the sweeping curves of the Danube. The refugees
were nearing the end of their journey. If Elisabeth
had climbed the boxcar wall to peer out, the view
that met her eyes would have been a lovely one.
Rolling, wooded hills, the edge of the great Bavarian
Forest, bordered the rich farmland surrounding the

city of Vilshofen-on-the-Danube.[1] Beyond the town
rose the green-bronzed domes of the twin-towered
Benedictine abbey. Close at hand, the Baroque
steeple of the *Stadtpfarrkirche*[2] soared above
rows of quaint old connected houses. As the city's
name implies, the waters of the great Danube
flow alongside the town on their way back to
far-off Hungary.

This place, beautiful as it was, became the
muddy, stagnant waters where the little uprooted
plant was submerged to soften and break it. The
Master Weaver sought a pure thread for His tapestry,
and sent the coming trials to prepare Elisabeth for
the beautiful part she would play in His plan.

The train pulled to a stop at the village
station of Girching,[3] six miles beyond Vilshofen. It
was December 2. The journey, with all its
eventfulness, lasted only one week.

The refugees climbed out of the train for the
last time. Uncomfortable as it had been, the
departing train was a tangible link with their old
life in Hungary. Now truly homeless, the refugees
turned to face the most pressing necessity of
their new life: finding shelter. Winter was
quickly approaching.

The villagers of Girching brought wagons to
carry the refugees into the town. The Bavarians gave

---

1   vils-hō'-fen
2   shtad'-far-kir-kuh; parish church. The original parish church of St.
     John the Baptist dates back to medieval times; after being partially
     destroyed by fire in 1794, it was rebuilt in the Baroque style.
3   geer'-hing

them temporary lodging in a large room inside a restaurant. Straw heaped on the floor made beds, and the families slept in a row, grateful to be together and to have a roof over their heads.

They had more cause to be grateful than they knew. The believers left Szárazd on November 27. On December 1 Soviet troops entered the village. Some villagers escaped with the last wave of retreating German soldiers, but many even then chose to risk staying home. The decision was a costly one. When the Red Army took Szárazd, the infamy of the Russian soldiers was tragically justified. The women had no defenders and now no escape. They were brutalized by the conquering men.

In early January, as in happier days, the drummer made the rounds of the village. This time his message was from the victorious Russians. Some families were given an hour to vacate their homes, and young people between certain ages were summoned to the town hall. Here, without warning, twenty-five of them were deported to forced labor camps in the Soviet Union.

All over Hungary, the same drama was repeated. Young ethnic German men and women were asked to report for a few weeks of *"málenkij robot,"*[4] "little work," such as clearing rubble. The innocuous request cloaked the implementation of top-secret Soviet Order 7161, which ordered the deportation and internment of all able-bodied

---

4    mah'-len-kee roh'-bət; from the Russian *malenkaya rabota*
     (маленькая работа).

German men between the ages of 17 and 45, and all able-bodied women between 18 and 30 from the Red Army's newly "liberated" territories. Hungarian collaborators led the Soviets to those who did not report as requested. If the expected quota of Germans was not met, the Russians made up the number with ethnic Hungarians or those outside the prescribed age range. Some of those taken were as old as 80 or as young as 13. In some villages, the entire adult population was deported. Those taken were marched to deportation centers, loaded into cattle cars, and sent to the notorious Soviet labor camps. Instead of a "little" clean-up work, the prisoners were forced into hard labor such as mining and road-building, under unspeakable conditions. An estimated 600,000 Hungarian citizens—400,000 prisoners-of-war and 200,000 civilians—were taken into the Soviet Union. One third died there. *"Málenkij robot."* The term became a bitter synonym for the terror and brutality of the Russian deportation.

Like many others, the young villagers of Szárazd were not allowed to return home before leaving. They had no chance to pack food or extra clothing, and the one outfit they wore when deported was small protection against the freezing winter. Work in the Russian coal mines was hard, and despite the exhausting labor and bitter cold the prisoners were given little water and minimal food. The small rations of bread were rock-hard, but they had to be eaten quickly or other starvation-gripped prisoners would steal them.

The suffering took a heavy toll on the young lives. One of Elisabeth's friends was among the many who died that winter. Her brother, also a prisoner, did his best to bury his sister, but in the frozen ground he could dig only a shallow grave. Under such cruel conditions, it is incredible that any survived.

The prisoners were released when they became too sick to work. Those who were freed struggled home to Szárazd. They were so weak that three or four nearly died before they reached it. Another of Elisabeth's friends arrived home emaciated, with her head shaved as all the girls' had been. As she stood on the street outside her home, her own parents did not recognize her. Those who survived bore scars they would carry for the rest of their lives.

Back in December, at almost the last minute before the Russians arrived, Opa Becht decided to flee. He was forced to leave empty-handed, as he and Elisabeth's remaining aunts and cousins fled in trucks with the evacuating German soldiers. The family dog followed the convoy, refusing to be left behind.

Their journey was far harder than the believers' had been. They reached Vienna safely, but were trapped there by the relentless Allied bombing. During one raid bombs exploded all around their shelter. Opa Becht ran into the street, calling desperately for the family to follow him. The Weaver's hand was at work again, and all survived.

After fleeing Vienna, the family wandered from city to city before they reached Passau in Bavaria. With no news of Elisabeth's family, Opa Becht planned to go back to Hungary to search for them. Before he left, a lady in Szárazd costume appeared in Passau. As the fellow-refugees talked, the lady realized that Opa Becht knew nothing of the community of Hungarians around Vilshofen.

"You don't know!" she cried in surprise. "Your daughter lives thirty kilometers ahead!"

Traveling quickly on to Girching, the once-wealthy Bechts arrived with literally nothing but the clothes they wore; even the beloved dog was lost along the way.

In the meantime, life in Germany was not easy for Elisabeth. The tapestry threads of those days were dark and hard ones. The family had food and shelter, but as December wore on they were unable to find a permanent home. Mother's tuberculosis closed door after door to the Wineckers; no one wanted to take in a sick woman. The Bavarian dialect made communication difficult, creating another barrier for the already openly-disliked refugees.

Mother grew worse, and Oma Winecker, like so many of the older generation, was broken by the trauma of leaving behind all she had ever known. Elisabeth, at fifteen, was forced to shoulder almost complete responsibility for the family. The girl who feared to go alone to Szárazd's quiet pastures now braved the hostile Bavarian streets, and carried on negotiations over paperwork at the city hall with a boldness that concealed her inner trembling.

At last a kind older couple agreed to take in the Wineckers. They owned a farm on the outskirts of Girching, and needed help with the heavy farm work. Hans, now twelve, was old enough to be a welcome help to the elderly farmer. A room over the stable was furnished with three beds, and the family gratefully moved in. It was an ideal situation for them, especially when Mother's tuberculosis forced her to enter the sanatorium in nearby Osterhofen[5] in January.

The farm couple supplied the family's basic food from the produce of the farm, including badly needed milk for little Kathi. Even so, the Wineckers were desperately poor. A French prisoner-of-war was assigned to help work the farm, and Elisabeth, now the breadwinner for the family, hired herself out for field work on the neighboring farms. Father's training stood her in good stead; she never thought the knowledge he insisted she learn would be so important so soon.

Oma Winecker did what she could. She went from farm to farm, telling the family's story and offering to spin the farmers' wool in exchange for a little food. Some of her hearers were sympathetic; others set their dogs on the despised refugee. When Oma was successful, she brought back a small loaf of

5   ōs'-ter-hō-fən

bread or a bit of ham to have on the table when Elisabeth came home. Those were red-letter days in that time of want.

Added to the other worries was the ever-present specter of war. The stress and fear that haunted the villagers in Szárazd followed them to Germany. Bavaria, rich in industry, was a prime target for Allied bombers. Fighters, too, prowled the skies. Trains, trucks—anything that moved—brought them swooping down, machine guns hammering. Even civilians became a target in this total war. Elisabeth and the farmers learned to drop flat in the fields at the approaching drone of aircraft. Once, on the way to visit their mother in the hospital, Elisabeth and Hans dove for shelter as an airplane strafed their train.

Mother's health did not improve, and at last she wrote to Father. The army commanders gave him leave to come for a visit in March, 1945.

The family knew he was coming, but not what day he would arrive. One afternoon Elisabeth was at a neighbor's house when she heard a commotion outside. Stepping out the front door to see what caused the noise, Elisabeth froze in shock: there on the street stood *both* her parents! Father had stopped at the hospital on his way and brought Mother home with him.

That week-long visit was a time to be savored and later treasured in memory. Together as a family once more, all the hardships dropped into the background. To relax, to shed the crushing responsibilities and become a child again, even for a few fleeting days, was inexpressible joy for Elisabeth. At the end of that beautiful week, Father had to return to the army. Elisabeth's frail little mother said good-bye to her husband for the last time. She never saw him again.

One night two months later, the little family huddled in the darkness of their one room, listening to an ominous roar approaching on the road. It was May, 1945. The invincible Reich was crumbling, and the Americans were invading Bavaria. A neighbor called the dreaded words a few hours earlier:

"Lights out! The Americans!"

Mother, home on a visit, had the children layer on all the clothes they had as a precaution. No one knew what was coming. Goebbel's propaganda machine had done its work, and the German people were prepared for hideous atrocities at the hands of the American soldiers. Only the lady who owned the little store in the front of the house was not afraid. She had a sister living in America, and declared there was nothing to fear from the Americans. As the rumbling tanks rolled closer in the blackness, her light was burning brightly.

The next day the city was in Allied hands. Elisabeth, horribly afraid and longing to be hiding at home, had to appear at city hall again. She hurried down the street, avoiding American uniforms in terror, and was enormously relieved when the errand was over. Little did she suspect that she would one day proudly call herself one of the Americans she held in so much dread!

Later that day, the more adventurous Hans and Heini returned home in great delight.

"The Americans are good!" they cried. "They gave us chocolate!"

Triumphantly they displayed an impressive array of gifts as they described the friendliness of the American soldiers. Elisabeth's fear left her, and it is a striking testimony to the American troops that, during the entire time Elisabeth lived in occupied Bavaria, she remembers nothing in their conduct that gave cause for complaint.

On May 8, V-E Day, the war in Europe officially ended. The conflict which for destruction and death stands unmatched in history was over, and the long road to reconstruction was about to begin. But from Soviet-held Yugoslavia, there was no word from Father.

# 7

## Cleansing and Pain

*"Seek the Lord, and ye shall live...*
*But let judgment run down as waters, and righteousness as a*
*mighty stream."*

~Amos 5:6

Waiting. How many other families, in those
first months after the war, waited in torturing
suspense for word of their husbands, fathers, and
brothers? For some, the word never came. For the
Wineckers, the long months of 1945 crept by in
heartbreaking silence. No letter, no news, no Father.

While the waiting and wondering hovered in
the background, the rest of life had to be carried on.
The surrender brought a welcome end to the
bombing and strafing, but Elisabeth's other
difficulties intensified. Mother was back in the
hospital, this time in an old converted castle in the
Bavarian forest. Since the new sanatorium was too far
away to visit often, Mother wrote little letters to the
children she loved so much. She never forgot their
birthdays, and always sent a card with her love to

each one. Those little notes, carefully saved, are some of Elisabeth's greatest treasures.

The language difference between the refugees and the native Bavarians was a continuing problem. The boys learned *Bayerisch*,[1] the Bavarian dialect, in school, and with the quick aptitude of children soon had no difficulty communicating. Hans

*Oma Winecker in Bavaria. Elisabeth is behind her.*

---

1  bie'-er-ish

in particular achieved fluency with astonishing speed. Elisabeth had finished her eight years of schooling before leaving Hungary, and struggled to master the new words and idioms. One morning a neighbor stopped by the gate and called to Elisabeth over the fence. The words made no sense. Elisabeth, still shy, asked the lady to repeat them. It didn't help. Much embarrassed, Elisabeth apologized; she would have to wait until Hans came home from school. That afternoon Elisabeth repeated the words to her brother, and discovered the worrisome sentence simply meant, "It's so cold!"

It was cold, and as winter deepened the cold increased. The sacks of clothing and supplies Mother hastily packed in Szárazd proved their value anew. The bare wooden walls of the unheated bedroom were thick with glittering white frost each morning, and the children huddled under Mother's thick comforter. With the bounding resilience God gives the young, they actually enjoyed the "snow" on the walls.

In the bleak economic situation facing post-war Germany, the family's poverty became acute. One day Oma Winecker faced her granddaughter accusingly. Fifty marks were missing; what did Elisabeth know about them? The accusation stung deeply.

"If I needed money, I would ask you for it," Elisabeth answered in quick anger. "I wouldn't steal your money!"

The tension dissolved when Oma discovered the lost marks in her own skirt pocket.

Trying to escape the worries at home, Elisabeth went with two friends to a nearby spot where Hungarian soldiers gathered. Evenings of dancing and singing were a welcome diversion for the music-loving girl, but while the company of the soldiers took her mind off the unpleasant realities of life, it left no lasting satisfaction. The little plant, stifled under dirty waters, could find no true escape.

One Sunday, the Szárazd believers invited their fellow refugees to a meeting. Elisabeth was one of the many who came. A carpenter offered his tiny workshop as the meeting-place. The believers swept up the shavings and everyone sat down. The little congregation had no pastor, so one of the elders from the village was the speaker that afternoon. As he began his address, his words went straight to Elisabeth's heart. He seemed to be speaking just to her. Elisabeth had known about God since she was a child, and she had heard of His love in sending His Son Jesus. She had heard, too, of the salvation He offered through faith in Christ's death and resurrection, but she had never put her trust in Jesus alone to save *her*.

Even as the man spoke, a battle began in Elisabeth's heart. The memory of the pleasurable evenings spent with the soldiers pulled her one way, and the call of the Lord pulled in the other. She was torn between the two. The struggle was sharp, but not long. The love of Christ caught hold of Elisabeth as it had the apostle Paul. There in the meeting, she gave her life to the One who gave His for her, and a golden thread of joy and faith began to shine among the dark threads in the Weaver's tapestry.

Elisabeth's conversion was part of a small revival that swept through the refugee community. Many who had persecuted the despised believers now repented and believed the gospel. An entire group of young people turned to the Lord. Elisabeth's mother, in her hospital bed, became a believer, and so did Opa and Oma Becht. Elisabeth's aunts also accepted the Lord.

With great joy, the church prepared for a baptismal ceremony. Baptism was not looked on with favor in Catholic Bavaria, so the ceremony was held quietly in the evening. The church gathered on the shores of the river, and with deep reverence the new believers were symbolically buried and raised with Christ in the waters of the Danube. The great river now became a symbol of the joy and new life Elisabeth had found in Christ. Cleansed by the blood of the Savior, the little plant was lifted from the muddy waters into the clean air above.

Like the sons of Levi responding to Moses' ringing challenge,[2] Elisabeth took her stand firmly on the Lord's side.

"I took that side, and that was the good side," she said, "and I'm thankful for that; otherwise how could I have done all that came after? There were a lot of things that were not easy."

---

2   Exodus 32:26

Elisabeth soon sorely needed the comfort and strength the Lord promises His children. The long-awaited letter bringing news from Yugoslavia arrived, but the handwriting was not Father's. The letter, dated November 30, 1946, was from Father's friend and fellow-soldier, who had returned to Szárazd after being released by the Russians.

The friend wrote that he and Father were in the same prison transport after they were captured. The transport left on the 11th of May. The prisoners were forced to march over thirty miles a day, often going five or six days without food or water. On the 4th of June they arrived at a prison camp near Belgrade. The next day the prisoners were divided into two groups. Father was sent with one group to another camp about 10 miles away, while his friend remained in the first camp with two other men from Szárazd.

Sickness ravaged the prisoners. On June 8th, one of the other men from Szárazd died. The friend himself was so ill that his weight dropped to 84 pounds.

In mid-July, a transport with sick prisoners arrived from the other camp. As the friend and his brother-in-law approached the truck, they heard a low, familiar voice calling them. It was Elisabeth's father. He was so pale and emaciated that his friends would not have recognized him.

"We will never see our homes or families again," Father told the two men. Then he told them

*The letter that brought the news of Father's death. The stamp in the upper left-hand corner marks the letter as passed by the military censors.*

that he had turned to the Lord. "He will make all things right," Father said.

The two men tried to bring Father bread and water, but when they returned the truck was gone.

Three days later, the friend wrote, his brother-in-law learned that Father was dead. He died in the camp hospital, and was buried in the German cemetery in Semlin.[3]

*This tiny snapshot is the last known picture of Elisabeth's father. It was taken on March 17, 1945, on his last leave in Bavaria. Mother's brother, Jakob Becht, stands beside him.*

Those words ended a year-and-a-half of uncertainty for Elisabeth. She had suspected it before, but now knew for certain that she would never see her father again. He had malaria, she learned, and in the delirium of fever he cried for his family constantly. Like his father before him, he lay buried in a mass grave in Yugoslavia. He was thirty-nine years old.

But that unmarked grave was robbed of its deepest sting. The letter said that Father had given his heart to the Lord before he died. Oh, the

---

3   Present-day Zemun, Serbia.

marvelous goodness of the Weaver's plan, in bringing those two friends to Father's side that day! A chance meeting, a brief conversation, and Father was given a chance to send his family a last word, a glorious message of hope: *"He will make all things right."* Father's victory had been won. He died looking forward to the triumph of the resurrection. What comfort that brought to the grieving daughter! But Mother must still be told.

Mother's brother and his wife, and her two sisters and their husbands took the letter to the hospital. That the news of Father's death came with the news of his eternal life was the great kindness of the Lord. When the family returned, they told Elisabeth that Mother had taken the news as a Christian should take it. High praise indeed for the lonely little mother. The God of all comfort was hers, and His consolations were not small.

Elisabeth, too, had a Comforter, but she desperately regretted that she had not honored her father more highly. She had often thought him hard and strict, but now realized how good he had been to her. Now that it was too late, she wished with all her heart that she could show him how much she loved him.

"Obey your parents," Elisabeth told the children who would hear this story, "because you don't know how long you will have them." She wiped her eyes with trembling hands. "You don't know it!" she repeated. "Really you don't. You need to appreciate them as long as you have them."

The thought that this was not the end, that someday both Father and Opa Winecker would rise from their unknown graves to meet the family in the air, was a blessed hope and comfort.

The family's bleak circumstances left Elisabeth with little time for grief, but those circumstances were now markedly different. The dreaded trips to city hall, the exhausting farm labor, and the grinding poverty were the same; it was an unseen difference that wrought the change. Inside Elisabeth, the Light of Life was now shining through the darkness.

An outward reflection of that light was the new joy Elisabeth found in the church. Sundays were now a cherished time to lay aside the responsibilities of the week and gather with the other believers from Hungary. Each week the small congregation filled the carpenter's workshop, sitting wherever they could find a place. In that rustic room, amid a company sincerely and purely committed to their Lord, Elisabeth found a blessed haven of glory and grace. The believers had been tried in the fire of persecution in Szárazd, and had, like Job, come forth as gold.[4] A spirit of hard-won faithfulness and practical holiness characterized the church; an atmosphere in which Elisabeth thrived.

Elisabeth and the other young girls in the church formed a close, fun-loving group. They, too, were dedicated to their Lord, and found ways to serve Him by serving those He loved. They started

4   Job 23:10

*Elisabeth (second from right) at a ladies' tea with church friends in Bavaria.*

an outdoor Sunday school for the children, and looked for ways to help support their families.

Elisabeth's second cousin, a cavalry officer in the Hungarian army who would later become pastor of the church, helped the girls in their task. Parachute cords, mementos of the hard war days, were abundant in Bavaria. Elisabeth's cousin collected and unraveled them. The girls dyed the silky fibers and knit them into men's vests. They took the vests to a nearby textile factory. New clothes were hard to come by, and the workmen were happy to exchange sheets, pillowcases, and blankets for the silk vests.

The girls also found ways to have fun while supplementing their families' tables. Wild blueberries grew in the Bavarian forest, and the happy group set off on a berry-picking excursion. Darkness fell before they got home, so they burrowed into a haystack for the night. Such trips were adventures, and Elisabeth's appreciation of a good time was as keen as ever.

"We had a lot of fun," she remembered. "So many to laugh with!"

Transportation was expensive, and several of the girls, including Elisabeth, learned to ride bicycles to help save money. Learning to maneuver the heavy, boys' frame bicycle was an adventure in itself. Elisabeth quailed at the memory, but Father's lessons in perseverance had not been in vain. She conquered at last, and the bicycle allowed her much more mobility.

The close community of the church, a family in the truest sense, was the Lord's gift to Elisabeth in the hard days that were approaching.

For some time, little Kathi had been moving one arm strangely while she walked. Elisabeth, busy with heavy responsibilities and little more than a child herself, didn't notice anything seriously wrong. One day the children went to visit their Aunt Katharina. Sharing the house with Aunt Katharina's family was a lady who had been a baroness back in Hungary. The baroness liked children, and on this visit she noticed Kathi's arm.

"That child doesn't walk quite right," she said.

*Bicycle riding with friends, on the way to visit Kathi in the hospital in Bavaria; Elisabeth is second from right.*

Then Elisabeth noticed it, too. They went immediately to Opa Becht, who took Kathi to the doctor in nearby Künzing.[5] The doctor agreed that something was wrong and said Kathi needed to see a specialist. Opa knew a specialist in Munich, the son of an old friend who was a doctor in Budapest, and took Kathi to him for testing. Tuberculosis had affected her spine. She was taken at once to the hospital and put in a full-body cast. For several years

---

5    kuin'-sing. the "ui" is pronounced halfway between "oo" and "ih."

*The Winecker family during the hard times in Bavaria. Kathi is in a full-body cast. This portrait is the only picture Elisabeth has of her mother.*

she was in and out of the hospital, and had to wear a corset for support when walking. In the Lord's grace, Kathi was eventually able to walk and run normally again. With intense gratitude, Elisabeth thanked the Lord who works all things for good to them that love Him.[6]

In August, the children went to the sanatorium to visit Mother on her birthday. Kathi

---

6   Romans 8:28

was with them, wearing her corset. Wildflowers lined the path as the four children climbed the hill to the hospital. As they came closer, they saw Mother coming down the path to meet them.

"Do you know who that is?" Elisabeth asked Kathi, pointing to Mother.

Poor little Kathi shook her head. "No, I don't know."

Heartsick, Elisabeth realized that Kathi hadn't seen Mother for so long that she didn't recognize her.

"Here, pick some flowers," Elisabeth said. "That's your mother!"

How the mother's heart must have ached when her little Kathi didn't know her! Mother was extremely careful of the children on their visits, not wanting them to come too close or stay too long, guarding them from the dreaded disease that was slowly claiming her life.

Day by day, the Lord quietly sustained Elisabeth, but there was more pain ahead for the little plant. After the *hanf* was lifted out of the pond, before it was worked, the roots were cut off. Elisabeth's strongest earthly "root," from which she drew a constant stream of love and care, was her mother. In the spring of 1947, it was increasingly clear that Mother was nearing the end of her earthly life. The tuberculosis was slowly draining her strength; the doctors could do no more.

In May, a pretty card arrived for Elisabeth's eighteenth birthday, written in Mother's delicate Old German handwriting:

"Happy Birthday! The Lord bless you. From your dearly loving Mother."

It was the last birthday card Elisabeth ever received. Through the fall and winter, Mother lingered on. The valley of the shadow was a long and hard one.

The doctors said Mother would not live past Christmas. As Christmas drew near, Elisabeth was constantly on edge. She jumped every time the door opened, afraid someone brought news of Mother's death. Her nerves were so frayed that one day as she ran to see who was at the door she tripped and fell headfirst down the stairs.

Christmas came and went, and still Mother suffered on. As the end drew near, Opa and Oma Becht took the four children to the hospital to say good-bye. Mother called them to her bedside. With infinite love she said good-bye to each one, and prayed over them.

Beside the words of love and prayer, Mother had a question for Elisabeth. Would she promise to take care of Kathi? Elisabeth solemnly gave her word. She knew the implications of what Mother asked, and accepted the responsibility as a sacred charge. Mother had the comfort of knowing that the little one she left behind would be cared for and loved. She knew Elisabeth would keep her word.

*Elisabeth's last birthday card from Mother.*

"And praise the Lord, *I did*," Elisabeth said, years after her promise was faithfully fulfilled. "That was not easy, but I did."

On January 22, 1948, Opa and Oma Becht were at Mother's side as she crossed the veil.

"She slipped away in peace," they told Elisabeth.

The little mother's journey was over; the crown of life was won. "Precious in the sight of the Lord is the death of His saints."

The day of the funeral was bitterly cold. Elisabeth remembered the solemn pilgrimages bearing loved ones to rest on Szárazd's hillside, and wanted to follow the coffin on its way to the

*The four children at Mother's grave.*

grave. The believers gently tried to dissuade her—the weather was too bad—but Elisabeth was determined.

"It is the last thing I can do for my mother," she said. All four children walked slowly behind the coffin on its journey to the cemetery.

Opa Becht paid for a beautiful stone marker. An English translation of the inscription reads:

*Here rests*
*Elise Winecker*
*born Becht*
*from Szárazd, Hungary.*
*Died after long and heavy suffering*
*on January 22, 1948,*
*in the 37th year of her life.*
*Mourned by 4 children.*

*Eternally united there,*
*Where none weep tears of parting sore;*
*Where we with countless multitudes*
*Will serve our God forevermore.*

*We will see you again!*

# 8

## *Softening and Scraping*

*"My heart rejoiceth in the Lord... There is none holy as the Lord: for there is none beside Thee:*
*neither is there any rock beside our God."*
~*I Samuel 2:1-2*

A year passed after Mother's death. The absence of that gentle though far-off presence left a new blankness in Elisabeth's life. Father and Mother were both gone, and the dream of a happy, reunited home was gone with them. The lonely years stretched ahead of her, offering no respite from the responsibilities that weighed so heavily. It was a dark time for the rootless little plant, but the Lord was gently washing and cleansing it. Silently, like the deep, quiet waters of the Danube, the comfort and grace of God flowed to Elisabeth's heavy heart. That never-failing stream carried the strength that kept her walking on. Without it, she would have crumbled under the burden.

The church was a bright spot in the darkness. Almost every day the believers gathered together, and Elisabeth went to every meeting. She faithfully attended the Bible study on Wednesday, the Thursday hymn singing, the prayer meeting on Friday, and the two Sunday services. The church became her second home, bringing her the Lord's encouragement and blessing throughout the week.

A team of young people, two boys and three girls, continued teaching the children's outdoor Sunday school. They met in the evenings to prepare each week's lesson, and those hours of reading verses and planning stories were joyful times. The Sunday school met at two o'clock in the afternoon—after dinner but before the three o'clock service—and one of Elisabeth's friends came every Sunday to help wash the dinner dishes so Elisabeth would be free to go. Elisabeth and the other young people loved teaching the children, and fully enjoyed those Sunday afternoons.

The church now met in the back room of a restaurant; a good location except when the kitchen crew turned up the radio until its blare drowned out the pastor. Visiting believers, such as a doctor from Budapest whose gifted preaching was long-remembered, brought cheer and hope with them.

Despite the encouragement of the church, the next few years brought a series of disappointments for Elisabeth. Her way seemed blocked wherever she turned. The Weaver was beginning to scrape the tough edges of self-will from Elisabeth's heart, leaving its fibers soft and willing in His hand. As God gently closed door after door, Elisabeth's eyes were fixed more and more firmly on His guiding hand.

*Elisabeth in her late teens, in Bavaria.*

Committing her way to the Lord meant leaving the direction to Him, and He did not always take her along the road she hoped. Following the Savior began to call for harder sacrifices, but Elisabeth was learning to wait in trust for His leading.

*The little Szárazd church in Bavaria, in front of the restaurant where they met for Sunday services.*

The first disappointment followed the visit of German believers who had traveled to America.

"America is wonderful," Elisabeth was told. "You can travel freely through the whole country. There are plenty of jobs; you can find work anywhere in America and earn a good salary."

At that time the dollar was worth four marks, or more. Travel restrictions and burgeoning unemployment haunted Bavaria and all of Germany. The glowing tales of freedom to travel and work awakened a great longing in Elisabeth. If only she could go to America! Her hope was quickly dashed; the American government would not accept unsupported orphans. The door was closed, but the Lord heard Elisabeth's desire. She was learning the secret of delighting herself in her Savior, and in His timing He would keep His word to give her the desires of her heart.[1]

The next closed door was harder still. A desire to work in foreign missions began to fill Elisabeth's heart. She longed to tell others about the joy and peace she found in Christ. One of the young men from Szárazd, a leader in the gang that persecuted the believers, had given his life to the Lord and gone as a missionary to Pakistan.[2] He returned to be married, and when he and his wife visited the church Elisabeth confided that she, too, wanted to go to the mission field. The answer she received was true, but hard to accept. Her responsibility was at home, caring for the children. That was her mission field. God had work for her there. Setting aside this second longing was not without a struggle, as the Lord began teaching Elisabeth to find joy serving Him at home.

A third path, the chance of nurse's training, was also blocked by Elisabeth's responsibilities at home. Elisabeth watched several girls, including her cousin, set off for nursing school without her. These were years of scraping and cleaning, working the fibers of Elisabeth's heart until they were ready for the Weaver to spin.

---

1 Psalm 37:4
2 This faithful man of God spent 40 years laboring in Pakistan, and his son is now continuing his work.

In the midst of disappointment, the Lord sent encouragement in unexpected and very practical ways. A man from Switzerland heard about the Wineckers, and began to send timely and useful gifts to the orphan family, including shoes for Hans and Heini.

Care packages arrived from America, and the believers traveled to Passau to pick them up. The girls were so nervous that they could hardly sign their names. Those packages were wonderful. Coffee, milk, cheese, butter...delicacies the refugees hadn't tasted for years. There were clothes, too: new dresses! The boxes were a treasure trove for those who had almost nothing.

The home God had given the family in Girching continued to be a blessing, but the farm couple was getting older. They had no children, so they took in a young woman from the wife's side of the family. She married while the Wineckers were there and eventually had two children. Although she was very kind—she and Elisabeth became lifelong friends—it was clear that the Wineckers could not stay on the farm forever. Elisabeth could not know it, but the Weaver was even then winding His shuttle with threads that would bring the family a home of their own.

A pitifully small number of the men from Szárazd slowly returned from the war, but devastated, overcrowded Bavaria offered few hopes of employment. One of the believers, Johann Trautmann, set off on his bicycle to look for work.

He was able to get a pass to the French zone, now the state of Baden-Württemberg. For over 200 miles he cycled through the countryside, searching in vain for any available position.

Riding one day under leaden skies, Johann had just passed the town of Riedlingen when rain began to fall. With what insignificant things the Lord does His work! Johann turned his bicycle back toward the town, and went to check in as required at city hall. The mayor was out, and the small-town clerk impatiently rebuffed the shabby refugee.

"What can I do with you? Go find the mayor."

Johann followed directions to the mayor's house, only to learn that the mayor was not at home, either. Out of pity for the rain-drenched stranger, the mayor's wife offered him a hot meal. Johann gratefully accepted. The lady set out the food, and noted with interest that the stranger reverently bowed his head before eating. His simple act had unforeseen consequences. Her curiosity aroused, the mayor's wife began asking the traveler questions. In the process, she learned not only his story, but that of the little Szárazd church. Johann's long trek in search of work added its own mute testimony to the hardships the refugees faced in Bavaria.

Johann's faithfulness in little things stood him in good stead again the next morning, as he dutifully returned to the city hall to present his papers and sign out of Riedlingen. This time the mayor was in, and the clerk sent Johann straight to the mayor's office.

The man Johann was about to meet was no
ordinary one. Ludwig Peter Walz[3] was elected in
1945 as the first post-war mayor of Riedlingen. As a
young man, Walz fought with distinction in the First
World War. He earned the Iron Cross, Second Class,
for his devotion to duty through such campaigns as
Normandy, the Somme, and Verdun. After the war
Walz opened a clothing business and became a
successful and respected merchant. A committed
Christian, he was an outspoken opponent of the
National Socialist policies of the thirties. His refusal
to serve under the Swastika led to repeated arrests,
but a Protestant pastor was able to secure Walz's
release on the grounds of Walz's Iron Cross. From
1934 until 1942, under cover of night, Walz drove
thirty-five kilometers to supply the nearby Jewish
community in Buttenhausen with food. Tragically,
the Jews he helped were sent to Riga and
Theresienstadt, but before their deportation Walz
provided each of them with supplies for the journey.
For his generous bravery he was later given the *Yad
Vashem* "Righteous Among the Nations" award. The
respect in which Walz was held was displayed by his
election, as a Protestant, to the office of mayor in an
overwhelmingly Catholic district. This, then, was the
man behind the door Johann Trautmann was about
to enter.

Mayor Walz greeted the refugee warmly. He
had learned the story of the Szárazd church from his
wife, and had an astonishing proposition for his

---

3   lood'-vikh pee'-ter vahlz

fellow believers. As mayor, he had the authority to grant them a tract of land near Riedlingen. The believers could build their own homes and church, and start a new life with their families.

"Send them to me," the mayor urged Johann.

That conversation was the beginning of a truly remarkable series of events. When Johann Trautmann brought the mayor's message back to Vilshofen, several of the other men traveled to Riedlingen. Mayor Walz welcomed them as brothers in the Lord, and showed them the tract of farmland he planned to give them. Along one border ran a small river lined with giant oak trees.

"I can see your houses there," the mayor said.

The Lord's provision was beyond anything the believers could have hoped for, but there remained one difficulty. In the late 1940's it was hard enough for one or two men to obtain a pass to travel between divided Germany's post-war zones. Permission for a group of 150 people to cross the border was unheard of, especially since the group included a family of unsupported orphans. It was madness to apply for anything so audacious.

The believers started praying. If this was the Lord's plan, He would see it through. Elisabeth's verse was on trial again. The believers were committing their way to the Lord and trusting in Him; would He bring it to pass? Still praying, they filed the impossible application for one hundred and fifty refugees, including Elisabeth's family, to cross the border into the French Zone.

The God who directs the hearts of kings like streams of water did His unseen work in the offices of West German bureaucracy. Incredible to all but the eyes of faith, the permits were granted. Jubilantly the little church prepared for the journey. They set out from Vilshofen-on-the-Danube and made their way toward the seemingly impassable border.

*"By my God have I leaped over a wall,"* David said,[4] and God brought the believers marvelously "over the wall." In perhaps the only instance of a legal group-crossing between the zones, the Szárazd church entered the French zone of Baden-Württemberg and continued toward Riedlingen.

One of the young girls fell ill along the way, and the caravan took shelter in the shell of a bombed-out town until she recovered. At last the believers entered the smooth, sweeping dale at the southern end of the Swabian Alps where Riedlingen lay. With the beautiful thoughtfulness of the Lord, a final touch to Elisabeth's new home wound its way down the center of the valley. Beside the half-timber houses of Riedlingen, as beside the streets of Vilshofen and the beloved hills of Hungary, flowed the wide familiar waters of the river Danube.

The believers arrived in Riedlingen in October, 1949. Once again the families were housed in various homes, and once again no one wanted the Wineckers. Finally they were given two small,

---

4   Psalm 18:29

*Elisabeth's cousin and a friend pose in a doorway in the devastated town of Weingarten on the way to Riedlingen.*

dilapidated rooms, a kitchen and a bedroom. Rats and mice ran up and down the walls. Elisabeth was terrified of the scurrying creatures, and her feminine fear was a temptation "her boys" could not resist. Hans and Heini teased her unmercifully.

"There's a rat!" they cried, and then burst out laughing as Elisabeth jumped up on a chair to escape.

Mayor Walz took a special interest in the orphan family, and brought them a goat. Elisabeth, still not terribly fond of animals, milked it faithfully, but the other children refused to drink the goat's milk. No one else wanted the milk, either, so the goat soon found another home.

Adjusting to life in Riedlingen meant yet another change in language for Elisabeth. The

Alemmanic Swabian dialect, *Schwäbisch*,[5] was different from that spoken in either Bavaria or Szárazd.

As the believers began building, the Lord's help was strikingly evident. None of the men were professional architects or had training in

*Construction crew at work in Riedlingen.*

---

5   shvay'-bish

Riedlingen contractor they did all the work themselves. They planned carefully, organizing themselves into a human assembly plant. The workers ranged in age from fourteen to seventy, and the girls joined in the construction work with the same enthusiastic dedication as the men and boys. The amount of work was staggering. Each of the forty-one cellars was dug by hand. The foundations were laid, the walls framed, and the roofs raised by hand. The believers moved like clockwork, working very nearly from dawn to dusk, as house after house slowly rose under the Swabian skies.

On Sundays, the church halted work and gathered for services in Riedlingen. They met in a *turnhalle*,[6] a gymnasium, close to the Danube River, during the two-year building period.

Another time of rest and celebration came in September, 1950, when the city of Riedlingen celebrated its 700th anniversary. The Szárazd believers joined the festivities, dressed once more in their colorful traditional costumes.

The land the mayor set aside for the church was a fifteen minute walk from the Wineckers' rooms, and each morning Elisabeth walked out to join the building crew. She and her friend Barbara (not the Barbara of the apple-hunting expedition) were assigned the job of carrying water from the stream to the cement mixer. In the midst of lugging the heavy water-buckets, Elisabeth's jokes and

---

6   toorn'-hall-uh

*Elisabeth in Szarazd costume at Riedlingen's 700ᵗʰ anniversary celebration*

cheerful conversation kept everyone around her in good spirits.

"Here comes the Winecker!" the other workers called when Elisabeth appeared. They were sure of a good time when Elisabeth was with them.

One blustery spring day, the workers were tired of fighting the weather and decided to take a break and have some fun. The men held the empty cement bags up to the wind and let them sail out over the field. Just then the new mayor arrived to see the building progress. He noticed the cement bags littering the field, and Elisabeth and Barbara ran out to drag them back. The embarrassment was not funny at the time, but after the mayor left the girls' sense of humor got the better of them and they laughed over the escapade.

Their work was hard, despite the times of fun and laughter, and each night Elisabeth returned to the little rooms in Riedlingen exhausted and terribly sore. Kathi still needed care, and cooking and cleaning waited to be done. Elisabeth was so tired that she often fell asleep at the table while Oma Winecker rubbed her back, trying to loosen the tight muscles.

"We worked *hard*, I tell you!" Elisabeth said as she looked back on those busy, satisfying days. "But

*Farmhouses in various stages of progress.*

we were young, we were happy together, and we did what we could."

"We did what we could." Elisabeth said it without pretension, but the accomplishment of that little group was extraordinary. In 1951, two years and an amazing 200,000 labor hours later, forty-one double houses stood on the land where Mayor Walz envisioned them back in 1949.

When all the homes were livable, the families cast lots for the houses. Each family's name was written on a slip of paper, and the church gathered around to watch the drawing. Seven of the forty-one homes were farmhouses, and Opa Becht dearly wanted his grandsons to be farmers. The very first paper drawn, for one of the farm houses, held the name "Winecker."

*An aerial view of the village of Eichenau.*

*The Eichenau church.*

"God is good," said one of the believers. "He gave the first home to the orphans."

The pastor loved to tell afterward how the "Father of the fatherless" had cared for His children. The Great Shepherd took care of His under-shepherd as well; the pastor's name was drawn for the house closest to the church.

The believers also chose the name of the new village by lot. "New Szárazd," "New Altheim," and other possible names were written on papers and one drawn out. The name chosen was a favorite with all the believers. They called the little settlement Eichenau,[7] after the spreading oak trees. As the families settled into their new homes, the work of the

---

7  ī'-ken-ow

Lord seemed wonderful beyond measure. They could say with the Israelites, *"Thou hast caused men to ride over our heads; we went through fire and through water: but Thou broughtest us out into a wealthy place."* *(Psalm 66:12).*

In the center of the new village the believers built a small, white church with a square tower, a symbol of simple, steadfast faith and gratitude. Of the millions of refugees who flooded West Germany, Elisabeth knew of no other group for whom the Lord provided so marvelously.

# 9

## Carding and Spinning

*"It is good that a man should both hope and quietly wait for
the salvation of the Lord...till the Lord look down, and
behold from heaven."*
~*Lamentations 3:26,50*

As the years passed, the Lord continued
quietly weaving. The threads of Elisabeth's tapestry
settled into a pattern of contented work and service,
for the Lord and for her family. Life in their own
home, though not one of luxury and ease, was much
better for the Wineckers. The family began to
receive some assistance from the government in
addition to Oma Winecker's small pension, and
Elisabeth continued her farm work.

The little village of Eichenau, with its
miraculous story, became a local attraction. Buses
brought visitors to tour the town. Mayor Walz always
brought the visitors to see the Wineckers' home, as a
testimony to God's care for His orphans.

One of the many visitors who came to the
Eichenau church was a believer from Switzerland.
His visit was particularly memorable for Elisabeth.

The Swiss man looked around at the many single young women in the church who were, especially by Szárazd standards, passing the normal age for marriage. Only three or four of the church's young men returned from the war, and these quickly married, leaving a generation of young women with little hope of a husband and family.

"Don't worry about it," the man told Elisabeth and the other girls. "You have a husband somewhere, and the Lord will take care of you until you get one." He looked around at them again. "Yes, the Lord has a man for you," he added with a smile, "but he just might be on the North Pole!"

Those words, half-jest, half-prophecy, lingered in Elisabeth's mind through the coming years.

The pastor also encouraged the girls to wait patiently and to learn to be contented in the Lord. "If you are not happy in Jesus," he told them, "you will not be happy married, either." The pastor knew what it was to be alone. Just after he returned from the war, his wife—Heinrich Frank's sister—died after a bicycling accident in Bavaria. She was expecting their first child.

The pastor, and the little Eichenau church, had a true evangelistic spirit. The believers invited the townspeople to evangelistic meetings, like the one in Bavaria that so deeply changed Elisabeth's life. At one of the meetings, the daughter of a wealthy factory owner accepted the Lord. As she listened to the pastor's message, she fell in love with the messenger as well as the Savior he represented.

*Elisabeth in her twenties, in Riedlingen.*

They were later married in a true union of love in the Lord.

Through the pastor's ministry in Riedlingen, Oma Winecker, too, found the way to the Savior. One day she met the pastor on the street and said bluntly, "I want to be saved."

"When?" he asked in pleasure.

"Right now," she answered, so they prayed right there on the street.

The church's influence spread beyond Riedlingen as the young people traveled by bicycle

*Evangelistic singing in Biberach, about 18 miles from Riedlingen. Elisabeth is fourth from the left in the front row, wearing her favorite red jacket.*

or bus to sing in nearby towns. Elisabeth loved singing as much as ever, and her alto voice added harmony to many duets. The youth sang an old German folk hymn called *"Gott sitzt am Webstuhl meines Lebens,"* "God Sits at the Loom of My Life," that beautifully matched the pattern of Elisabeth's tapestry:

*"God sits a-weaving at my life-loom;*
*He holds the threads within His hand.*
*And not in vain He crafts the pattern,*
*To make it please Him, strand by strand.*
*Though strange to me it sometimes seemeth,*
*When so confused the threads He plies,*
*His arms will never sink or falter,*
*While He the weaver's shuttle guides."*

The Weaver guided His shuttle without
faltering as He wove a new thread into Elisabeth's
tapestry. The pattern He set for her followed the
path of the Savior, and Elisabeth had to learn again
to echo the words of the Lord Jesus: "Not my will,
but Thine be done."

The Weaver's new test began at a Christian
youth meeting in another town, where a young man
noticed Elisabeth.

"That is my little wife," he said to himself.

The young man spoke to the uncle of one of
Elisabeth's friends, and arranged a meeting with
Elisabeth at her friend's home. The church had strict
standards for conduct between young men and
young women; young couples were not allowed to be
alone until they were engaged. Wanting time
together, the young man and Elisabeth met in the
woods to talk, and Elisabeth told him the story of her
life. Before long she had a ring on her finger and the
engagement was announced.

As they talked about their coming marriage, a
problem arose. The young man told Elisabeth that
he was willing to have Kathi live with them, but not
Elisabeth's brothers or her grandmother. After many
discussions, Elisabeth wrote to tell him that he was
welcome to come live in their home after the
wedding, but that she could not leave her family
alone. They were her responsibility under God; she
could not leave them. In his return letter, the young
man broke the engagement. Elisabeth took off her
ring, honestly happy that the engagement had been

broken on his side. Like her father, she sacrificed her hopes to her duty, though the struggle was not an easy one.

Another heart's desire was taken away, another door closed, and another lesson in patient trust begun. The fibers of Elisabeth's heart needed more pounding and softening before the Weaver was ready to join them with another thread in marriage, but this fourth desire was not forgotten. Like the other three, it would find a beautiful fulfillment in the Weaver's perfect timing.

The years rolled on, and Hans and Heinrich finished school. Neither of them, to Opa Becht's disappointment, wanted to farm, so the farmhouse was traded for a home in the village and the boys were trained as auto mechanics. Kathi, too, grew up, and left home to pursue her dream of becoming a teacher.

When the boys began earning salaries, the government revoked the family's financial assistance. The loss of the monthly sum, small as it was, meant that Elisabeth was no longer able to support herself on the low-paying farm labor. She would have to look elsewhere for work. A more serious consequence involved Oma Winecker, whose declining health would not allow her to be left at home alone during the day. The Lord provided a solution through Oma's widowed daughter, Elisabeth's Aunt Annamarie. Annamarie lived with her son and daughter-in-law in another town in West Germany, and she offered to care for her aging mother.

Hans, Heinrich, and Elisabeth accompanied Oma on the drive to her new home. Poor Oma! For the third time, she had to leave all she knew. Her distress was so great that her grandchildren were afraid she would die before the drive was over. They had no other choice—Annamarie's offer was a true blessing—but it was terribly hard for Oma.

Once the hardship of the move was over, Oma was happy with her daughter's family. Annamarie's son owned a television set, the first Oma had ever seen. In the middle of a movie, Oma got up and left the room. She came back wearing one of her Sunday dresses. Puzzled, the family asked her why she had changed her clothes. Oma replied, "They can see me, too."

She thought the people on the television could see out just as well as she could see in. When Oma was born in 1881, the telephone and light bulb were in their infancy, and the Benz Patent-Motorwagen was still five years in the future. What inventions and innovations came and went during Oma's eighty-five years! From the first automobile to amphibious tanks, from the dunes of Kittyhawk to manned space flight...no wonder Oma didn't know what to make of the modern marvel of television.

Annamarie took loving care of her mother until 1966, when Oma went to join her husband, her son, and her Savior in the eternal home she would never leave behind.

Now alone in the home in Eichenau, Elisabeth taught kindergarten for a year in the beautiful new building built by the church, and then found a job in the fabric-printing factory owned by the pastor's father-in-law.

The Lord now began to send the tension of persecution to strengthen His thread. After several years at the fabric-printing factory, Elisabeth transferred to a factory that made fine enameled cookware. She was one of the only Christians working there, and her belief in the Bible was a subject of recurring ridicule. One man in particular mocked Elisabeth's faith. She quietly held firm, but the factory was not an easy place to work.

Elisabeth became good friends with one of her coworkers, a Catholic girl from Riedlingen. She often visited her friend's home, and this opened the way for a new time of testing. Elisabeth's friend had a brother, and he often happened to be home when Elisabeth came visiting.

"We didn't fall in love," Elisabeth said, "but we liked each other."

The young man was not a believer, but Elisabeth pushed that out of her mind. It was so hard to be alone. By this time the Lord had fulfilled the Swiss visitor's prophecy for many of Elisabeth's friends, and in her loneliness Elisabeth thought that perhaps this marriage could be the Lord's will, too.

Over the next few months the friendship grew, and Elisabeth began to fight with herself. Her friend's brother did not know the Lord, but he attended the Catholic church. Elisabeth knew they would not be allowed to marry unless she became a

*The new kindergarten building in Eichenau.*

Catholic. She could not in good conscience accept the teachings of the Catholic church, and she knew the misery of a marriage when husband and wife are walking different paths. One woman back in Szárazd had accepted the Lord while her husband remained an unbeliever, and Elisabeth had seen the anguish of the mother who longed to bring her children up to know the Lord.

"What communion hath light with darkness?" the Bible asks, bidding Christians not to be "unequally yoked" with unbelievers.[1] Like the unmanageable cows in the wheat field so many years ago, two lives following different "furrows" could not truly work together.

---

1 II Corinthians 6:14

Elisabeth knew what she had to do. She could not sacrifice her faithfulness to the Lord and His Word, even for the companionship she longed for. But oh, the pull of the flesh was strong. It was the same battle Elisabeth had faced that Sunday in the carpenter's workshop, the same battle faced by all who follow the Lord. The Lord won that first fight by His love, and in His strength the battle was won again now.

After a funeral which Elisabeth and the young man both attended, Elisabeth had the opportunity to say the words she had fought against so long. On a street corner in Riedlingen that stands vividly in her memory, Elisabeth told her friend's brother that she could not see him any longer. She explained why very simply, and they did not meet again except in passing.

Elisabeth later looked back on that decision, hard as it had been, with unmixed gratitude.

"I would say to every young lady—I have the opportunity now—don't marry a boy who is not a Christian, when you are a Christian," Elisabeth said. "I warn you—really—you can love him, you can...oh, but that is not the right thing to do."

One day not long after, Elisabeth was walking home when she saw the pastor heading in her direction.

"Let's go for a walk, Elisabeth," the pastor said.

Elisabeth agreed, and they set off. The pastor was kind, but direct.

"I've heard that you have been meeting with a young man who is not a believer," he said. "Is that true?"

Elisabeth acknowledged that it was.

"What would happen if you got married?" the pastor asked.

"I knew I would have to become a Catholic," Elisabeth said, and told him how she had broken off the relationship.

The pastor's honest, straightforward approach in this and other matters left an indelible impression on Elisabeth. When he heard there was a problem he came straight to her. He spoke to her face rather than behind her back, and his kind but uncompromising counsel did more than all the whispers of gossip and backbiting. The lesson of speaking face-to-face with brothers and sisters, in truth and in love, was one that Elisabeth would carry with her for the rest of her life.

The Weaver was carefully guarding His handiwork in Elisabeth. He wanted a pure, strong thread for His weaving, and to strengthen it further He gave it work to do for Him. Elisabeth continued teaching Sunday school, and found joy watching the children grow in the Lord. She prayed for each of the girls and boys she taught, and rejoiced as she saw them grow up to serve the Lord. One of her students was the daughter of her old friend Elisabeth Schell, now Elisabeth Wenzel. When the Wenzels moved to America, Elisabeth gave her pupil a pretty teacup and a good-bye letter. Little Elisabeth kept that cup

*Elisabeth (second from left) and friends in Szárazd costume in Riedlingen. The three girls on the left (all named Elisabeth) are wearing costumes that belonged to Elisabeth's mother. On the right, the pastor's second wife, Ursula, is wearing one of Elisabeth's costumes.*

and letter, and still treasures them after more than fifty years. She would have another part to play in the pattern on Elisabeth's tapestry, but that was still far in the future.

Elisabeth and a friend also started a new *Jungschar*,[2] a Bible club, to teach young girls Scripture verses and songs. One summer Elisabeth hosted a week-long girls' camp; the house was filled with laughter and fun, but with serious study about the Lord as well. At the end of the week the girls gave presentations of what they had learned, and the pastor was so impressed that he made a film of their

2   yung'-shar

accomplishments. Those were happy times, and Elisabeth laughed as she remembered how the years had flown. Those little girls of yesterday are great-grandmothers now!

For nine years Elisabeth worked in the unfriendly atmosphere at the cookware factory, and gained a firm foundation in the art of standing alone. While the Weaver strengthened His thread, He made ready to fulfill one of her early desires.

The great change about to take place in Elisabeth's life was completely unsuspected. Her beloved pastor held a Bible study for Christian nurses in a nearby hospital, and the love and care they gave their patients greatly impressed him. When he heard that the hospital planned to open a nursing school, he thought of Elisabeth. He knew of her struggles at the factory, and of her earlier dream of being a nurse.

"I found a place for you," he told her at church. "A new nursing school is being opened in Münsingen,[3] and I think you should go."

Elisabeth was less confident. Nursing school? It was almost thirty years since she had been in a classroom, and her only education was eight years of elementary school back in Szárazd. How could she go to nursing school?

But with the pastor's encouragement, Elisabeth applied to the new nursing school in Münsingen. She was accepted. The Weaver was

---

3  mu in'-sing-ən; "ui" halfway between "oo" and "ih."

ready to add a new color to His tapestry, and
Elisabeth was apprehensive but full of anticipation.

Before classes began, Elisabeth took her first
overseas trip, to visit her aunt in Canada. Oh, that
first plane flight was an adventure! Elisabeth
discovered that she loved the thrill of traveling,
flying, and seeing new places. She relished the
flight over the Atlantic and the time with family
in Canada.

Shortly after her return to Riedlingen,
Elisabeth left for nursing school. She took with her a
small wooden plaque, a gift from Kathi. Three words,
painted in white on the golden-brown wood, stood
out clearly: ER KANN HELFEN – "He can help."
Elisabeth committed her way to the Lord once again.
Her trust had never yet been disappointed.

It was 1969 when Elisabeth arrived in
Münsingen to begin her studies. She was glaringly
out of place among the educated young girls that
formed the rest of the class. They were in their late
teens or early twenties. Elisabeth was forty years old.
As classes began, her lack of education was painfully
apparent. She was terribly behind the other
students. The worst task of all was German
composition. Most of her early grammar and writing
classes were in Hungarian, and writing technical
papers in German taxed her mind to the breaking
point. The difficult, involved subject matter
threatened to overwhelm her, and the medical
supervisor did not expect her to finish the year.

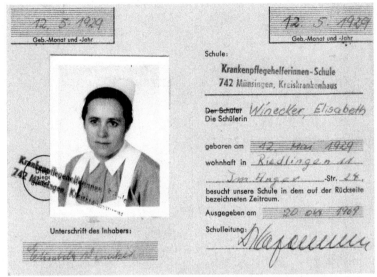

*Elisabeth's nursing* Schülerausweis[4], *student identification card.*

Determined to succeed, Elisabeth threw herself into her studies with desperate energy. She had "all the treasures of wisdom and knowledge" in Christ,[5] and in His strength she persevered.

Outside the classroom, the students rotated through the hospital departments to gain experience in each area of nursing. Elisabeth learned to treat infections, assist in the operating room, and perform a multitude of other required tasks. She also had to learn not to mind being ordered about by the younger nurses!

The surgical recovery ward was Elisabeth's favorite; the people she cared for there got well and

---

4   shui'-ler-ows-vice; "ui" halfway between "oo" and "ih."
5   Colossians 2:2-3

*Elisabeth (back row on the left) and her fellow nursing students strike a light-hearted pose during the busy days in Münsingen.*

went home. So many of the others didn't. That was hard part of nursing: the patients they couldn't save. Some faces, in the Lord's mercy, soon passed from Elisabeth's memory. Others she never could forget. Those were the hardest.

There were hard things outside the school as well. Near Münsingen, deep in the forest, was a sinister furnace left from the days of Nazi horror. During the war, truckloads of Jews were transported here secretly at night. The German people living nearby did not find out until after the war what that strange smell in the night had been. Back in Bavaria was the concentration camp at Dachau, but Elisabeth had not had any idea of the unthinkable "final solution" being carried out there. She and her brother visited Dachau years after the war, and were appalled at what had happened there. Though the camp was in the same state where they had lived, its grim wall of barbed-wire seemed worlds away.

The struggle inside the school continued as the months passed. The year-long training course was a marathon of intense mental effort and discipline. The Weaver's thread was being stretched in earnest, and sometimes Elisabeth thought her mind was as *kaput* as that long-ago train engine. *"Er Kann Helfen,"* Kathi's little plaque reminded her, and Elisabeth held on. At the end of the term, the Lord rewarded Elisabeth's determination by doing the impossible once again. The "hopeless" student passed every exam, and cleared the first hurdle on the road to becoming a registered nurse.

With the training course completed, Elisabeth was qualified to work as a nurse's assistant. She decided to gain more experience before taking her registered nurse's exam, and the Lord quickly provided an opportunity. Leni,[6] a nurse who worked with Elisabeth at the Eichenau kindergarten, knew several nurses who worked at a hospital in West Berlin. She suggested that Elisabeth apply for a job there. Elisabeth was accepted for the position, and set out to begin work in the divided German capital.

---

6   Pronounced halfway between lay'-nee and len'-ny; nickname for
    Helene or Magdalena.

Shortly after Elisabeth arrived in Berlin, she went for a walk down a wide city boulevard. It was a rainy day, and not many people were on the sidewalks. When Elisabeth returned from her stroll, her patients asked where she had gone walking. Elisabeth told them, and the ladies were horrified.

"Don't you know what street that is?" they asked.

Elisabeth, new to Berlin, didn't, but the patients quickly informed her of its infamous character. It was no street for a woman to be walking alone. The heavenly Father of the fatherless had His protecting hand over His daughter that day.

At the Berlin hospital, Elisabeth discovered a great love for her new work. The Lord had directed her into a profession perfectly suited to her personality; she simply loved caring for people. She was assigned to a floor with arthritis patients, and the steady, settled work was exactly what she liked best.

One of Elisabeth's patients was a young mother from East Berlin. She and Elisabeth became good friends, and when the lady's term in the hospital ended, she invited Elisabeth to come visit her. Life was hard in East Berlin for a wheelchair-bound mother with a young son. Elisabeth well remembered the years of poverty and want in Bavaria. She knew what it was like to scrimp just to have food on the table, and what it meant to have some treat, however small. Remembering the wonder of those American care packages, Elisabeth filled a bag with *wurst,* cheese, noodles, and other delicacies unavailable in East Germany. Friends warned her that customs would charge her steeply to allow the food into East Berlin. Elisabeth committed the bag to the Lord, and prayed that if He wanted her friend to have the food, He would allow her to cross the border without paying an exorbitant price.

Elisabeth rode the train to the Communist border, and waited in the customs line with her bag. When she reached the guard, she set the bag down to show him her passport. The guard checked her papers and waved her through, asking no duties for the food at all. *"He shall bring it to pass!"* The Lord's promise held firm. Elisabeth's friend and her son were delighted with the gift. The people of East Berlin had very little, and the bag was a treasure for them.

Elisabeth spent two years in Berlin before returning to Riedlingen. After another year of preparatory work in the hospital there, she began commuting to a hospital in Zwiefalten,[7] about seven miles away. She had a new skill to help her with the commute. At 42 years old, on the busy streets of Berlin, Elisabeth had learned to drive. Piloting her little white *Kadett* was a new adventure that Elisabeth greatly enjoyed, whether she was driving across Germany or simply to work and back.

The Zwiefalten hospital brought Elisabeth experience in an entirely different field: psychiatric nursing. The new position was challenging. Some of

---

7   zvee-fah lt'-en

the women were insane; others had alcohol addictions or suicidal tendencies. Elisabeth still enjoyed her work, but it could be nerve-wracking at times. The women had to be watched constantly, and some were fiendishly clever.

Once, while Elisabeth supervised a group of patients in an outdoor courtyard, she turned around to find one girl missing. Hastily Elisabeth scanned the yard. The girl was nowhere to be seen. The fence ran unbroken around the perimeter, and there was no other exit. Where had she gone? The hospital staff searched everywhere, while a shaken Elisabeth worried and prayed. Thankfully the missing girl was soon found. In the few moments Elisabeth's back was turned, the girl had dropped into a shallow drainage ditch and wriggled through the eight-inch gap under the fence to the outside.

Despite the difficulties of the job, Elisabeth remembers her time in Zwiefalten with much pleasure. The other nurses were closer to Elisabeth's age than the girls in Münsingen, and they bonded into a close group of friends. The camaraderie between the nurses led to much fun and good fellowship.

While working at the psychiatric hospital, Elisabeth was able to afford the luxury of a bit of traveling. Packing her suitcase, she headed off to various destinations around Europe on her vacations. In 1973 she journeyed to the Black Forest town of Donaueschingen[8] to see the source of the Danube

---

8  doh-now-esh'-ing-en; *Donau* is the German name for the Danube.

River. She loved the mountains, and on one trip to Austria she went hiking in the Alps. The lonely beauty of the mountain peaks thrilled her. Suddenly, miles up the trail, a man accosted her. His manner frightened Elisabeth.

"How would you like to go pick Edelweiss with me?" he leered.

Elisabeth, alone and with no help in sight, gave a decided, "No!" and was terribly relieved when he walked on. A few moments later, to Elisabeth's horror, he returned. As he approached her, two girls with a sheep beside them appeared on the trail.

"Where did they come from?" the man demanded angrily. The trail was empty moments before. Elisabeth, weak with relief, answered truthfully that she didn't know. But as she made good her escape, she was very sure she knew who sent them.

"The Lord protected me. Literally the Lord protected me," she said. Elisabeth still doesn't know how the Lord arranged for the girls to appear at just that moment, but she marveled at His care for her.

"I was not such a good girl," she said, "oh, but He was good to me."

God had indeed been good to the village girl from Szárazd. In February, 1976, Elisabeth took her final nursing examination. She was horribly nervous. During the oral portion of the exam her mind went blank on the difference between cataracts and glaucoma, and she was in tears after the test. Her nervous confusion lowered her final grade,

*Elisabeth's beloved little German Bible.*

but the student expected to drop out of her first year of training left the examination hall as a registered nurse.

The Lord's years of carding and spinning had not been wasted. His careful hands had changed Elisabeth from a timid girl into an earnest, capable woman. Her confidence in the Lord's power had grown as she watched Him work, and her love for His Word had grown as well. Her little Bible was marked throughout with verses the Lord had made special to her. The fear of the Lord and the knowledge of His word were bringing her the wisdom the Bible promises. She served her Lord in love and gratitude, and her selfless service earned her the love and gratitude of those around her.

The character of the child left its echoes in that of the woman. The unknown was still frightening, and unexpected situations still jangled her nerves. Elisabeth had never fully recovered from the strain leading up to Mother's death, but she was learning to meet challenges in the Lord's strength. She was still quiet and reserved around strangers, but her early timidity had been lessened by stern necessity, and a frank, outspoken manner had taken its place. In fact, outspokenness was her new struggle, and her quick tongue sometimes caused her trouble. Accustomed for years to taking responsibility, she made decisions quickly and sometimes impulsively. Her sense of humor was thoroughly intact, and her warm, loving loyalty to her friends was as firm as ever.

Elisabeth's life was a rich and happy one. Her days were filled with satisfying work, the fellowship of the Eichenau church, and joy in the Lord. Still, the Swiss visitor's prophecy lingered in her memory. "The Lord has a man for you..." Was it true? Did the Lord have someone for her, even on the North Pole?

# 10

## *A Matching Thread*

*"He will keep the feet of His saints."*
~*I Samuel 2:9*

The morning the letter arrived began like any other. No inkling warned Elisabeth that the day would be any different from the one before or after it. When Heini brought her an envelope that was delivered to his house by mistake, Elisabeth had no way of knowing that it would change her life forever. Though the postmark was not from the North Pole, the letter was, as Elisabeth said dramatically, "from *him!*"

"He" was Edmund Blischke,[1] a man with a story as amazing as Elisabeth's own, and one remarkably similar. Edmund, too, was born in a small village close to the Danube River, but many miles farther down its winding course, close to the Black Sea. His family lived and farmed in the little town of Mathildendorf,[2] Romania, perilously close to the Soviet border.

---

1   blish'-kee
2   mah-till'-den-dorf; present-day Zhovtneve, Ukraine.

Though in Romania, Mathildendorf was a German town. Like Elisabeth's family, the Blischkes traced their ancestry back to Germany. They were *Bessarabiendeutsche*,[3] descendents of ethnic Germans who were invited by Tsar Alexander I to farm the region of Bessarabia, which he had newly acquired from the Ottoman Empire. Edmund's parents, Jakob and Emilie Blischke, were born in Bessarabia, under the reign of the tsars and the domain of Russia. After the Revolution of 1917 swept away the refined but ruthless Nicholas II and put the Bolsheviks in power, the Bessarabian parliament voted to declare independence from Russia and join Romania. Russia refused to recognize the vote, but the region came under Romanian control. The rest of the turbulent twentieth century saw further changes in the region, and today historical Bessarabia is divided between the countries of Moldova and Ukraine. In a strange twist of political history, Jakob and Emilie were born in Russia, their son Edmund in Romania, and their birthplace is now owned by the Ukraine.

Mathildendorf lay in the "Breadbasket of Europe," and the Blischkes' black soil was so rich that they needed no fertilizer. As in Szárazd, the animals were trained to leave their stalls when released in the morning and join the herds in the street for the walk to the pastures. Like Elisabeth's grandfather, the Blischkes farmed with horses. Instead of the threshing machine or the flails, they threshed their wheat with a concrete roller. A slowly

---

3   bess-a-RAH'-bee-en-doi'-chuh; literally, Bessarabia-German.

*Farmland surrounding Mathildendorf, with view of Neu Mathildendorf (present-day Novosilka, Ukraine) just across the river.*

walking horse pulled the heavy cylinder in a circle around a central post, crushing the kernels from the ears of grain. Wheat, barley, and oats were all threshed with the horse-drawn roller, which was much faster and more efficient than Elisabeth's well-loved flails.

Another useful crop grown in Mathildendorf was a pretty, slender-stemmed plant with bright yellow flowers. The seeds, roasted and crushed, yielded a healthy cooking oil. The plant grew in Szárazd, too, but it wasn't used for oil there; Elisabeth's father sent her to pull the yellow-flowered "weeds" out of their fields!

Sunday was a special day for the Blischke family. They walked to church in the morning, and after the service friends and relatives gathered at the

Bundesarchiv, Bild 183-W0402-500
Foto: Dissmann I Juli 1944

*These slant-sided wagons are similar to those the Blischkes used.*

Blischkes' home to share a meal and enjoy invigorating conversation. Jakob and Emilie's faith in their Lord was firm and vibrant, and in the years to come their oldest son Edmund was to watch that faith rewarded in remarkable ways.

In Romania, as in Hungary, political clouds began to gather as the 1930's came to a close. On June 26, 1940, the Soviet government issued an ultimatum to then-neutral Romania, laying claim to Bessarabia and demanding the withdrawal of all Romanian forces. Romania felt it unwise to object, and on June 28 the withdrawal began. The Red Army moved forward with lightning speed. Within a week, Russian troops occupied the regions of Bessarabia, Northern Bukovina, and Hertza.

With the Soviets suddenly in control, all Mathildendorf prepared to flee. The village had been captured by the Russians during World War I, and that terrible time had never been forgotten. The Russian troops had rounded up every man they could find and deported them to Siberia. None ever returned.

The Russians made no protest as the villagers gathered supplies and loaded wagons. The Germans' unhindered flight was part of a delicately reached political agreement. In a secret protocol of the Molotov-Ribbentrop Pact (1939), the Nazi and Soviet governments placed Bessarabia in the Soviet "sphere of influence." Russia agreed to allow the unmolested resettlement of Bessarabia's approximately 93,000 ethnic Germans to the new territories of "Greater Germany." The *Bessarabiendeutsche*, including the Blischkes and their extended family and friends, became pawns in the intricate drama of German-Soviet relations.

The Blischkes left Mathildendorf on October 4, 1940. It was the first of three times that the family would walk away from everything they owned. Twelve years would pass before they again had a home they could call their own.

In the first of a series of miracles, Jakob returned home in time for their flight. His army guard post had been overrun by the Soviets, but his knowledge of the Russian language enabled him to escape by masquerading as a Russian civilian. He and the other village men left Mathildendorf a week before their families, driving wagons filled with food and personal belongings. Everything else the Blischkes owned, including their beloved dog Donau, named for the Danube River, had to be left behind.

"We left everything, and glad we could go," Edmund remembered. "Otherwise we would end up in Siberia later."

Such fears were far from groundless. In the first year of Soviet occupation, over 50,000 people of various nationalities were deported from the former Romanian territories. Had they remained, the *Bessarabiendeutsche* would likely have joined their countrymen from Hungary in the dreary, deadly archipelago of Soviet concentration camps.

Emilie and the five children traveled on buses provided by the European Lutheran Church to the Danube River. A ferry carried them up the Danube to Brahova, Yugoslavia, where they expected to meet Jakob. Day after day went by with no sign of the wagons from Mathildendorf. After six weeks in the refugee camp, they were ordered to move on. The family journeyed on to Czechoslovakia, where they found shelter in an old convent. Here Jakob miraculously found them. The German army had commandeered the wagons and horses, and he had been forced to travel on foot. It was the Lord's special mercy that the family was reunited.

The Blischkes applied for German citizenship in Czechoslovakia. When they took the required medical examinations, the Lord worked marvelously again. How marvelously, they would discover later.

*Edmund as a boy.*

Edmund's younger sister Lydia was born without most of her fingers and toes, and the doctor scrutinized her abilities carefully before allowing her to pass. In Hitler's quest for a genetically pure "master race," any defect was ruthlessly suppressed. The family learned later of many who entered the examination rooms never to reappear.

Hitler's resettlement plan sent most of the *Bessarabiendeutsche* to the regions of East and West Prussia in northern Poland. The Blischkes were taken to Ritterwall,[4] in north-central Poland, and given an appointment as caretakers on a farm confiscated from the Poles. For three years they lived in uneasy peace, under the shadow of veiled hatred from the displaced Poles and the threat of a coming Soviet invasion.

Edmund was fourteen when he received a draft notice from the Third Reich. Emilie, horrified, burned the paper. Before the notice could be served, the Red Army forged into Poland on its push for the Nazi capital, and the Germans had no time to concern themselves over one draftee. "All things for good," the Lord promised,[5] even the dreaded Russian invasion. Later Edmund realized what the Lord spared him from. Most of the young men from his region were sent to defend Germany's last stronghold, Berlin. Had the draft notice been served, Edmund would likely have joined them in the Reich's hopeless and bloody final stand against the Allies.

On January 20, 1945, two days after the draft notice arrived, a horseman galloped into the Blischkes' farmyard. He shouted for the family to leave immediately. The Russians were close behind him. Faced again with the ugly threat of Communism, the Blischkes once more found themselves on the run.

This time their flight was made under desperately difficult conditions. The winter of 1944-

---

4   Present-day Bogusławski, Poland.
5   Romans 8:28

45 was one of the coldest in European history. The long lines of refugees suffered horribly. Many succumbed to exposure and disease, and their loved ones were forced to leave them behind in the snow, unable to bury them in the frozen ground. Historians estimate the number of German citizens fleeing the Soviet advance at 4 to 5 million. Between 600,000 and 1.2 million perished along the way.

Edmund's family, too, was touched by tragedy. Emilie gave birth prematurely to a baby daughter. They named her Renate,[6] "rebirth." In the harsh conditions, she lived only fifteen days. The Lord's kindness provided not only a casket but a place in a nearby churchyard for little Renate.

*A scene from the "Flüchtlingstreck," the refugee flight from Poland.*

---

6   rə-nah'-tə

Bundesarchiv, Bild 146-1979-084-05
Foto: o.Ang. | März 1945

*This line of refugee wagons in East Prussia would have followed the same route as the Blischke family.*

Despite the cold, the ground in the churchyard was soft enough for Edmund and his father to dig a small grave. Edmund's uncle preached the gospel at the graveside service, and many passers-by stopped to listen. In those uncertain days, when death dogged every step, each in the gathering crowd was offered God's gift of rebirth. Little Renate's short life gave each of those listening a chance to gain life eternal. Who can say how many of them will meet her someday in the land "beyond the skies"?

Though that terrible winter brought sorrow and grief, the Lord used even the numbing cold to protect His children. If the weather had been less severe, the family would never have escaped at all. A succession of rivers, small and large, lay between the refugees and safety. The retreating Germans had literally burned their bridges behind them in a desperate attempt to halt the Russian advance. In other years, the family would have been trapped between the icy waters and the vengeance of the Soviet soldiers, but in that fiercest of winters the rivers froze. The Hand that divided the waters before the children of Israel had lost none of its power. As the east wind opened a path through the Red Sea, so that freezing winter bridged the rivers of Europe. Edmund never forgot the Lord's deliverance, and counted the miracle of the ice bridges as great a wonder as the water-walled corridor of the Exodus.

The ice was too thin for the wagons, so during the night the refugees built "bridges" out of straw. They spread a swath of straw on the ice, wide enough for a single wagon, and poured buckets of water over the straw. The water froze before morning, thickening the ice enough to allow the wagons to pass. The crossings were still perilous. Wagons were carefully spaced to avoid overloading the ice, and stakes marked the path of safety. Edmund heard stories of wagons that strayed off the path and crashed through into the icy water.

At last the Blischkes reached the broad expanse of the Elbe River. On the other side of the Elbe, they had been told, lay safety. Miraculously, a bridge still spanned the river, and the family hurried to the other side. They were among the last to cross the bridge; German troops destroyed it two hours later.

Five miles beyond the sheltering barrier of the
Elbe, the Blischkes' journey ended in the tiny town
of Pattensen.[7] The mayor assigned them lodging in
the home of a wealthy couple. Already sheltering two
other families, the Blischkes' hosts resented the
large new group of unwelcome guests. The pretty
plains of Lower Saxony had been inundated by a
flood of refugees. The population of little
Salzhausen, just south of Pattensen, nearly doubled.

Germany was still very much at war. Bombing
raids on Hamburg, sixteen miles to the north,
brought terrifying explosions day and night. When
the war ended and the Allies partitioned Germany,
Pattensen was in the British Zone, a mere twenty
miles from the Communist border. Once again, the
Lord's protecting hand was over His children.

In Pattensen, as in Bavaria, the shortage of
housing and work was critical. The number of
refugees in Europe in 1945 is conservatively
estimated at thirty million. Almost six million
displaced persons lived in the American and British
zones of Germany alone. The economy was
shattered, and all money issued during the war was
worthless. Edmund watched British soldiers pull
handfuls of coins from their pockets and roll them
jangling into the gutter. No one stopped to pick
them up.

It was during the hard times in West
Germany, though, that Edmund made his parents'

---

7   In 1972, Pattensen was incorporated into the larger town of Winsen,
    Germany.

*The Blischke family.*

dauntless faith his own. Along with three of his sisters, he put his trust in Jesus Christ for salvation. Edmund stayed true to that decision for the rest of his life. He had watched the Savior protect him from great earthly danger, and now trusted Him to bring him safely to the "city which hath foundations, whose builder and maker is God."

In 1952, the Lord worked marvelously again. The Blischkes were sponsored through the Baptist World Alliance to come to America, a rare thing for so large a family. Here they found a home after twelve years—from 1940 to 1952—as homeless refugees.

Edmund had been trained as a machinist in West Germany, and moved to New York to find work. In 1954 he married Erika Woelper, the daughter of long-time friends. The couple moved to southern California, and God gave them three children: Heidi, Rosemarie, and Bobby.

In 1975, tragedy again touched Edmund's life when he lost his wife Erika. A year after her death, Edmund wrote to his younger brother Armin, who had settled with most of the extended Blischke family in Brookfield, Wisconsin. It was hard to live alone, Edmund wrote, and he felt he was not managing well with the children. Did Armin know anyone who would be good for him?

With the Lord's intricate interweaving of lives, Armin had married a girl whose parents were from a small town in Hungary, not far from the Danube River; a small town named Szárazd. In fact, he had married Elisabeth's former Sunday school student, Elisabeth Wenzel's daughter Elisabeth.

When Armin's Elisabeth heard that Edmund was hoping to marry again, she immediately thought of her family's beloved friend, Elisabeth Winecker. In 1969, Armin and Elisabeth had traveled to Germany to visit family and friends, and Elisabeth Winecker had liked Armin so much that she asked jokingly if he had any brothers.

"Yes," Armin replied, understanding her joke, "but they're all married!"

Armin's Elisabeth called Elisabeth's aunt in Canada to ask for Elisabeth's address, and found that she still lived in Riedlingen. Keeping her own counsel and saying nothing to Elisabeth's family, she gave Elisabeth's address to Edmund. Excitement in Brookfield began to run high—among both the

Blischkes and the Wenzels—at the possibility of those two, both devoted to the Lord, both so well-loved, being joined together.

And so the letter from "him" arrived. Elisabeth couldn't believe it. She was forty-seven. Someone wanted to marry her now, at forty-seven? The thought tickled her sense of humor. Like Sarah, she laughed at the thought of the Lord's blessing coming at her age. Still laughing, Elisabeth called a friend over and showed her the letter. They read it together.

"Oh, I don't know. I don't know," Elisabeth said as they read. The thought of being married after so many years seemed ridiculous. Besides, she would have to leave home, family, and friends. No, Elisabeth decided to forget about it.

As they washed dishes together in the church kitchen that Sunday, Elisabeth's friend asked her, "Did you write back?"

"No," said Elisabeth, still amused at the thought.

"Why not?" her friend asked in surprise. "You're planning to go to Canada to visit your aunt anyway. Why not write and see what happens?"

Elisabeth's friend had married a widower, and her encouragement made Elisabeth think more seriously about the letter she had whimsically dismissed. Could this be the man God had for her? The timing was perfect. She was about to go to Canada, and she even had her visa for America. Her nurse's training was complete. Her responsibility to her family was at an end. Oma Winecker was with the Lord, Hans and Heini were both married and established in their careers, and Kathi, her special charge, had finished her education and was engaged to be married. The promise Elisabeth had given at her mother's deathbed had been fulfilled.

After much prayer, Elisabeth wrote back to Edmund. They corresponded, but still Elisabeth was unsure. Edmund was a godly man who loved the Lord, and Elisabeth's heart yearned over the motherless children. She did not hide from herself her growing feelings for this man in America, but she simply didn't know if this was God's plan.

It was decided that Edmund would travel to Canada to meet Elisabeth while she was there. *"Commit thy way unto the Lord..."* The verse had proved true so many times, and Elisabeth had learned the importance of prayer.

"Lord, give me a 'yes' or a 'no,'" she prayed. "Just let me be sure. I don't need to be married. I'm a nurse; that is what I want to be. But if this is Your will, I will do it."

Praying for guidance, Elisabeth packed her suitcase and headed for the airport at Stuttgart.

# 11

## *The North Pole*

*"I will not let thee go, except thou bless me."*
*~Genesis 32:26*

Elisabeth arrived safely in Canada, and greatly enjoyed the time with family and friends there. When she contacted Edmund to arrange their meeting, he asked if she would be willing to come to California instead. He would pay her fare from Toronto and back again. She could meet the children, see the house, and get a better idea of what life would be like in America. Elisabeth readily agreed, but the change of plans led to an unexpected problem. Edmund and Elisabeth had never met, or even exchanged pictures. How would they find each other at the airport? They came up with a novel solution to the dilemma: Edmund would wear a green suit when he came to meet her, and Elisabeth would wear a green dirndl, the German folk costume.

When the time came to leave Canada for the trip to California, Elisabeth put on her dirndl as promised. The costume was a pretty one. The dark green skirt and vest were edged with dainty pink embroidery, and the white, short-sleeved blouse was gracefully gathered at the neck. Elisabeth tied the pale pink apron around her waist. Today she might meet the man the Swiss visitor spoke of so many years ago. Who could say? She had flown close to the North Pole on her way to Canada. Well, she had committed the matter to the Lord; she was waiting for His answer.

Elisabeth's family came to see her off at the Toronto airport. As they walked through the terminal, they teased her about her arrival in California.

"When you see the seven green suits at the airport," they said, "make sure you pick the right one!"

They speculated on various mix-ups with green-suited gentlemen as they accompanied Elisabeth to her gate. Still laughing, they called after her, "Pick the best one!"

After a stopover in Chicago, Elisabeth arrived at the small Ontario Airport where Edmund was supposed to meet her. Remembering the teasing back in Toronto, she scanned the waiting crowd nervously. Here she found a problem that had never entered her mind: not one man in that airport was wearing a green suit! Elisabeth stood helplessly on the red carpet while the other passengers greeted their family and friends and began bustling away. Still no green suit. Isolated by her complete lack of English, Elisabeth picked up her suitcase and followed the departing passengers.

As she was about to give up hope, she saw him. He came hurrying toward her, green suit and all. The sound of good German words was music to Elisabeth's ears. Edmund had been detained at work and was very apologetic.

What he did next, Elisabeth remembered with a smile, was the thing that "caught" her. In it she heard the Lord's unmistakable "yes." Edmund said, "Let's sit down and pray."

Sunny southern California was a far cry from the North Pole, but the Swiss visitor's prophecy had finally come true.

Edmund took Elisabeth home, and introduced her to the three children. Heidi, the oldest, spoke a little German. Rosemarie and Bobby spoke only English, but though talking was difficult they got along well together. Elisabeth had loved the children before she met them, and they soon liked her, too, as children usually did. Edmund's mother was visiting, and she welcomed Elisabeth warmly. Edmund himself was just as he had seemed in the letters that brought Elisabeth thousands of miles to meet him. Everything pointed to a happy end to the visit, but there was a time of testing ahead.

When Edmund inquired about a permanent visa for Elisabeth, he was informed that the quota for immigrants from Germany was full for the next two years. When Edmund told Elisabeth about the quota, she was upset. Two years? In two years she would be almost fifty.

"Forget it!" she said impulsively.

Edmund didn't "forget it," of course, but Elisabeth felt instinctively that waiting two years was not God's will. Had she been wrong? Was the Lord telling her that Edmund, much as she cared for him, was not the man He had for her after all? Elisabeth was convinced that God had given her His "yes" at the airport, but she was just as convinced that the Lord did not want her to wait those two years. She dared make no promise without the Lord's further leading. Edmund was too godly a man to press her into a decision, and at the end of the week nothing was settled between them.

Edmund drove Elisabeth back to the airport. As they walked into the terminal together, Elisabeth realized that they still had no picture of each other.

"We need to have a picture," she told Edmund, "to remember this. We don't know if we'll ever see each other again."

A passer-by took a picture of them together with the airport tarmac in the background.

Elisabeth returned to Canada, and Edmund returned to work. He told his supervisor about the unexpected barrier of the two-year quota.

"Have her apply as a fiancée," the supervisor suggested. "That goes much faster."

Edmund called Elisabeth, still in Canada, and told her what the supervisor said. With the two-year question out of the way, Elisabeth had the Lord's peace again. She would apply as a fiancée as soon as she got home.

*Edmund and Elisabeth's first picture together, before the uncertain parting at the Ontario Airport.*

When Elisabeth got back to Germany, she waited until all the friends who had come to greet her went home. She needed to talk to her brothers alone.

When Elisabeth was finally alone with her brothers, she told them that she had decided to move to America and marry Edmund Blischke. She can still see Hans and Heini standing there, shocked.

*The picture that Edmund sent to Germany for Elisabeth's pastor to see. Counterclockwise from right: Edmund, Heidi, Rosemarie, and Bobby.*

"You can't do that to us!" they said. Elisabeth was like a mother to the two brothers she called "her boys." They didn't want to see her move halfway around the world. "If you have to get married," they pleaded, "you can get married here!"

"I've made up my mind," Elisabeth said. "It is the Lord's will. I'm going."

Hans and Heini weren't the only ones that didn't want Elisabeth to leave. Her aunt and uncle also thought she was making a mistake, and warned her about the difficulties of being a step-mother.

Elisabeth listened. She knew the coming adjustment would be difficult, but she was sure of her Lord's call.

When Elisabeth went to the hospital agency to give them her resignation, the supervisor tried to change her mind.

"You really want to go?" he asked, and Elisabeth said she did.

"Here," he said, "I'll give you a raise." He had the document on his desk, hoping to entice her to stay. "Do you still want to go?"

Elisabeth was firm. When he saw that he couldn't change her mind, the supervisor tore the paper in half and threw it in the trash basket.

Elisabeth's beloved pastor was cautious as well. He wanted to be very sure what situation Elisabeth was going into. Edmund sent Elisabeth a picture of himself and the children so the pastor could see it. As the pastor got to know Edmund, he not only gave his blessing to the marriage, but came to truly love Edmund as a brother in the Lord.

Elisabeth applied for her green card, and traveled back and forth to Stuttgart for the required medical examinations. By October, five months after her return, her documentation was complete.

The final good-byes were terribly hard, and Elisabeth was grateful that the Lord's "yes" had been so clear. Without that solid confidence that she was following her Lord's will, she never could have left Germany. Hans and Heini took her to the airport that last day in Frankfurt. The parting was

wrenching, for her and for them. They all wept, and
Hans was so moved that Elisabeth was afraid his
heart would give out. When Edmund picked
Elisabeth up in Ontario, she was still so shaken that
he hardly recognized her.

Elisabeth arrived in California on October 17,
1976, and on October 30 she and Edmund were
married at the German Church in Los Angeles.
Mama Blischke sewed the plain satin wedding gown,
and Elisabeth wore a single, large orchid on her left
shoulder. Heidi was Elisabeth's maid of honor, and
Ernst Woelper, Edmund's first wife's brother, was
best man. Edmund and Elisabeth walked down
the aisle together. The German pastor performed
the wedding service, and pronounced them man
and wife.

"What God hath joined together, let not man
put asunder." The Weaver's time had come. He had
remembered Elisabeth's early desire for marriage,
and now He beautifully joined His two threads
into one.

The brothers and sisters at the German
church dearly loved Edmund, and joyfully arranged
the wedding. They provided the cake, food, and
flowers, and did all they could to make the
day special.

Despite the showers of love and kindness,
Elisabeth's wedding day was a heavy time for her.
There was no loving family to watch and rejoice with
her. Father and Mother were gone, and it was too far
for anyone to travel from Germany. Of all Elisabeth's

*Edmund and Elisabeth on their wedding day, October 30, 1976.*

many friends, not one was there that day. The faces that filled the church, though so friendly, were still the faces of strangers. Elisabeth was new to everyone, and everyone was new to her. Even her bridegroom was new; they had only been together a few weeks. All the American wedding customs were so different from the well-loved Szárazd traditions. Cutting the cake—and feeding it to each other!—was one of many new and strange experiences for Elisabeth that day.

After the wedding, the new couple set off on their honeymoon. The wedding day had been draining for Elisabeth, but the week alone with Edmund in Palm Springs was wonderful.

Elisabeth's deep love for the mountains was unchanged, and one day the newlyweds went for a hike together along an Indian trail. Edmund warned Elisabeth about a California danger that didn't exist in Europe: rattlesnakes. The trail led along a little desert stream. Elisabeth was hiking in front as they came up to a tree, and as she took a step she saw a snake just beyond her foot. The snake was as startled as she was. Elisabeth jumped back.

"Edmund! A snake!"

The snake disappeared before Edmund saw it, but they decided to finish their hike on another trail. Later the same day, they saw a row of snakes preserved in jars at an Indian museum. Elisabeth stared at one of them.

"That's the same snake that I saw!" she told the museum guide. It had been a rattlesnake, a very venomous one, and Elisabeth could praise the Lord once again for His protection.

That week began a life together for Edmund and Elisabeth that would last for thirty-five years. There were hard times still ahead, but the Lord was with them in those trials as He had been in the past. Psalm 37:5 was still beautifully true. Together, Edmund and Elisabeth committed their way to the Lord, and He brought His good pleasure to pass over and over again.

# 12

# *A Threefold Cord*

*"Now therefore let it please Thee to bless the house
of Thy servant...for Thou blessest, O Lord,
and it shall be blessed for ever."*
~*I Chronicles 17:27*

The Master Weaver had twined Elisabeth's thread with Edmund's, and the third pure strand of the Lord's love bound them together in the "threefold cord" that is not easily broken.[1] The cord needed the Lord's strength, because the first years of Elisabeth's life in America were not easy ones.

After that first wonderful week together, the happy couple returned to Upland. Edmund's mother had stayed with the children during the honeymoon, and she stayed afterward to spend time getting to know Elisabeth. Mama Blischke's warm love and rich Biblical counsel was a great blessing to the new bride, and their friendship was soon deep and close. Her presence was even more welcome because Elisabeth had few others with whom she could speak

---

1   Ecclesiastes 4:12

German. The children understood a little German,
but, except for Heidi, they didn't speak it at all. For
the fourth time, Elisabeth had to learn a new
language, and she found English a much harder task
than the first three. She had been a child when she
learned Hungarian, and the Bavarian and Swabian
dialects shared many similarities with her native
German. English was far more difficult.

Edmund went back to work at the Johnston
Pump Company, and Elisabeth settled into life as a
*hausfrau*,[2] a housewife, and mother. The adjustment
was not easy, for Elisabeth or for the children. It was
especially difficult for eighteen-year-old Heidi, who
had taken her mother's place to the two younger
children since their mother died. It was not easy for
her to relinquish the position, and for Elisabeth to
have to take it from her was equally hard. Elisabeth
loved the children dearly and never meant to be
strict or harsh, but her own upbringing had been a
rigid one, and she was far more strict than the
average American mother. With the language barrier
added to all the other difficulties, there were some
very, very hard times. In the Lord's grace,
today Elisabeth's relationship with her children—
they are always and emphatically *her children*—is one
full of love.

"I am so thankful that today, we are a family,"
Elisabeth said. "We live like any family. I praise God
for that."

---

2  hows'-frow

*Edmund at his work on the machine lathe at the Johnston Pump Company. The camera seldom captured the twinkle-eyed humor so characteristic of Edmund's personality.*

Other things made the first months after the marriage difficult as well. In November, back in Germany, Elisabeth's aunt went to visit Mother's grave. When she reached the cemetery, the beautiful headstone, and the grave itself, were gone. Land in Germany was limited, and families had to pay a continual rate to keep a grave intact. Opa Becht had paid for a certain number of years, but even though they had not expired, the church had needed the space and the grave had been removed.

Elisabeth's aunt called to give her niece the news. "It is like you took your mother with you," she said.

The thought of that quiet resting-place, so sacred in a daughter's eyes, being rudely disturbed, was hard to bear. Now Mother's grave was unknown, too. In the midst of the hard-hitting adjustments to life in America, this new grief seemed doubly hard. Elisabeth clung to the Lord. He knew where that dear little mother lay. Mary Magdalene, too, sorrowed over the supposed violation of her Loved One's grave.[3] Elisabeth set her eyes on the truth that flooded Mary's grief with unspeakable joy: the glory of the resurrection. When the great trumpet of the Lord sounded at the last day, Mother—along with Father and Opa Winecker—would hear the glorious call no matter where she lay.

As the months passed, Elisabeth began to gather friends around her as she had in Szárazd and in Germany. The Blischkes attended Foothill Baptist Church in Upland, and Edmund's church family welcomed Elisabeth with open arms and a love she never forgot. The friends at the German church in Los Angeles were not forgotten, and the Blischkes drove there for Christmas and other special occasions. The friendships formed in those early days in America remain a great source of joy to Elisabeth today.

---

3   John 20:11-16

At Christmastime that first year in California, Ruth Ogman, a lady from the Upland church, planned a special surprise for the new Mrs. Blischke. She invited Elisabeth to a ladies' Christmas tea, and also invited Ilse, the wife of her husband's coworker, who spoke fluent German. When Elisabeth walked in, Ilse greeted her in German. It was a breathtaking surprise.

"I could talk German!" Elisabeth said, rapturous at the remembrance. "Do you know what that was for me?"

Leaving the strain of forming English sentences behind, Elisabeth talked with glorious freedom. She and Ilse became good friends, and eventually gathered a group of German-speaking ladies around them. The friends met regularly at each other's houses for a real old-fashioned German kaffee-klatch.[4]

In 1982, Elisabeth's friend and her husband came from Germany to visit. While they were there, on the morning of May 5, Edmund left for work as usual at six o'clock. Elisabeth drove down to the post office to mail a letter for him, and when she got home Bobby told her that the pump company had called. Elisabeth returned their call, and was stunned at their message. Edmund was in the hospital. He had had a heart attack.

Elisabeth couldn't believe it. The visitors came hurrying out of their room, asking what was wrong.

---

4   kah'-fee-klatch; a friendly get-together over coffee.

"Edmund had a heart attack," Elisabeth said in shock. She got ready to leave at once for the hospital.

"We'll go with you," her friends said, and Elisabeth was grateful they were there. They drove with her to the hospital, where they found Edmund very weak. His arm had started hurting when he arrived at work, and the pain got rapidly worse. The man on night shift was the only person there, and Elisabeth always counted his presence a great blessing. Edmund was planning to drive home again, but the workman insisted he should call the ambulance. Edmund gave in, and was taken at once to the hospital around the corner.

That night Elisabeth and her friend talked as they cleaned up the kitchen.

"What would you do if something happened to Edmund?" the friend asked, wondering whether Elisabeth would go back to Germany.

"I would stay here," Elisabeth replied. "This is my family now. I would stay here; I wouldn't go back."

The Lord's kindness didn't leave Elisabeth alone again in a strange land. Edmund's condition stabilized, and after three or four days he was moved to another hospital. When Elisabeth visited him, she was appalled at the noise and bustle. Compared to the hushed halls of German hospitals, the American hospital sounded like a restaurant.

"Oh, come home," she told Edmund. "I'll take care of you."

Soon enough, she was able to bring him home and care for him herself. Edmund returned to work after he recovered, and the Blischkes' life went on with a new gratefulness to the Lord for leaving them together.

Two years after Edmund's heart attack, Elisabeth completed the requirements for American citizenship. On November 16, 1984, the United States issued a Certificate of Naturalization to Elisabeth Blischke, and she became an American citizen. The Lord had remembered the young girl's longing to come to America. He had promised that if she delighted herself in Him, He would give her the desires of her heart, and in His time He fulfilled her desire in a way she never dreamed possible.

No, the Lord does not forget. Three of Elisabeth's desires He had beautifully granted. Only one remained: her dream of work as a foreign missionary. This, too, the Master Weaver was fulfilling. He sent His thread to America, to bear testimony there of His love and work. Elisabeth's day-to-day life was a testimony of its own, but the Lord gave her a chance to speak more publicly and specifically for Him. The wife of one of the pastors at the Upland church heard Elisabeth's story, and organized a women's meeting so others could hear as well. In front of a group of foreigners in a foreign land, the German girl bore witness to the power and faithfulness of her Lord. She told of His unfailing provision, His strength in sorrow, and His glorious redemption. Echoing her mother's practical love,

*Edmund and Elisabeth in front of their well-traveled Volkswagen van.*

Elisabeth knit a basketful of *paschke* for the ladies
who came to the meeting.

In this book, too, may the Lord fulfill that
last of Elisabeth's desires: that through her, others in
faraway lands might come to know the joy and peace
she has so fully found in Jesus Christ.

Edmund's long-standing job was interrupted
when the Johnston Pump Company moved to Texas.
They invited Edmund to move with them, but he
and Elisabeth didn't want to leave their home and
their children. Heidi, Rosemarie, and Bobby were all
married, and Edmund and Elisabeth were alone in
the Upland home. How different from the
loneliness of Eichenau, though, because they were
alone *together.*

Finding another job proved more difficult than Edmund expected. He was older now, and no one wanted to risk hiring a man who had already had a heart attack. The years before Edmund was old enough to retire were lean ones. He could find only sporadic work, and though he and Elisabeth were both accustomed to getting by with very little, they had a hard time making ends meet.

After Edmund retired, the Blischkes had a small but steady income. Because their wants were few, they were able to save enough to indulge their love for traveling. They crisscrossed the United States, from Ellis Island to San Francisco, visiting historical sites and points of interest across the country.

Their travels took them to Europe as well, visiting friends and family in Germany. The visit to Riedlingen was bittersweet for Elisabeth. Some of the Eichenau friends had become quite prosperous, even wealthy, but in their affluence they had drifted from the Lord. Like the children of Israel, they followed God in privation and suffering and saw Him do miracles on their behalf, but in prosperity they forgot Him.

Looking in distress at the changes in her friends, Elisabeth realized why the Lord had her leave Germany. If she had remained in Riedlingen, a well-paid and respected registered nurse, it would have been hard to keep her footing on the Rock as her friends drifted away. The adjustments in

America had not been easy, but they had kept her eyes on her Lord.

"When you lose everything, then you turn to the Lord," Elisabeth said, "and when you have everything again, you forget Him. That's how that goes. And I praise the Lord, I didn't forget Him, and He took care of me."

When the fall of the Soviet Union left Hungary free, Edmund and Elisabeth traveled back to visit Elisabeth's birthplace. As the bus rumbled closer to Szárazd, Elisabeth grew more and more nervous. She hadn't seen her hometown for almost fifty years, and a flurry of emotions gripped her.

When she saw the street sign pointing the way to Szárazd, she begged the bus driver to stop so she

*The first sign of home, turning off the main road on the way to Szárazd.*

*Elisabeth with the first childhood friend she met on her return to Szárazd.*

could take a picture. She could hardly contain herself as she and Edmund walked into the village. The first woman she saw was an old friend. As they went along Elisabeth recognized face after face, and what exclamations of surprise as they recognized her! With joy they renewed friendships half-a-century old. Elisabeth took Edmund up to every house and introduced him to one old friend after another. That afternoon the cows came walking up the village street, just as they did when Elisabeth was a child.

At last they walked up to the farmhouse that Elisabeth had last seen on that dark Sunday in 1944 when she turned her back on it weeping. The house was in good repair, with flowers blooming along the drive. Elisabeth went up to the door she had locked

in grief so long ago. When she explained to the
woman that opened it that the home was her
birthplace, the woman warmly invited her in. The
rooms looked different, of course, and were
decorated beyond the means the Wineckers had in
Elisabeth's childhood. The farm, too, had changed.
Father's pigsty and corncrib had burned soon after
the family fled, but to Elisabeth's surprise the little
wooden outhouse was just the same.

That visit to Szárazd was a wonderful time of
nostalgia and fellowship, but it was not without pain.
Near the church a memorial had been erected to
those from the town who perished in the war.
Elisabeth laid her finger beside her father's name.
No, Szárazd was not the same, and never would
be, but how good God had been in the years that
had passed.

The Master Gardener had nourished His little
plant in Szárazd's rich soil, and uprooted it with His
loving hand. He left it in muddy waters until it was
ready to submit to His working, and then tenderly
washed and cleaned it. Scraping and pounding,
though painful, prepared the fibers for His skillful
spinning, and the supple, strong thread fully justified
His patient labors. He then twined His thread with
another, equally well-prepared, in a union of
marvelous unity and joy. Truly He had done "all
things well."

*"Commit thy way unto the Lord; trust also in Him,
and He shall bring it to pass."*

"That word is *true*," Elisabeth said earnestly. "I trusted His word from sixteen years old until today, and He made everything *right*, in my life. I went through many hardships, we went through many hardships; ah, but the Lord, He did it good. I give God the praise for all that we went through."

That is Elisabeth's prayer for this story of her life: that the Lord would have the praise and glory that He deserves for His work. Elisabeth never saw herself as an extraordinary person, and seldom talks about herself unless asked. Everyone has a story, she says. It is the Lord's work, His loving care for His fatherless children, and His unfailing faithfulness to His word that make Elisabeth's story remarkable.

As Edmund and Elisabeth left Hungary, Elisabeth saw another sign along the roadside. She loved it so much that she had to stop and take a picture of it, too:

VISONTLÁTÁSRA![5]
GOOD-BYE!
AUF WIEDERSEHN![6]

Elisabeth's beloved country bid her farewell in the three languages of her life: Hungarian, English, and the language closest to her heart, German. As we close our exploration of the Lord's beautifully woven tapestry, the meanings behind those three phrases

---

5   vee-sohnt-lah'-tash-rah
6   owf vee'-der-zane

*Good-bye in three languages.*

are Elisabeth's prayer for each one who has "met"
her through the pages of this book:

Until we see each other again, may God be
with you, and may we see each other at last in
the great crowd redeemed by the blood of the
Lamb. *Auf wiedersehn!*

# Epilogue

*"The joy of the Lord is your strength."*
*~Nehemiah 8:10[1]*

*"Be thou faithful unto death,*
*and I will give thee a crown of life."*
*~Revelation 2:10*

The years passed quietly in Upland, and Edmund and Elisabeth grew old together in harmony and love. As traveling became less practical, they enjoyed staying at home, walking the shady streets and greeting neighbors who were now old friends. They loved the local library, a privilege not always available in Europe, and Edmund researched topic after topic in the history that fascinated him. The Blischkes still had little, but they were used to that, and they were rich in friends, family, and in the grace and love of the Savior. Day by day they followed the Lord together, simply enjoying each other's company.

---

[1] Elisabeth marked this verse shortly after Edmund's death, and the verse from Revelation was given to her at her confirmation.

In the early part of 2012, Edmund and Elisabeth were both in poor health. Edmund grew steadily weaker, and in May he was hospitalized. His great desire was to come home. A hospital bed was set up in the living room, and on Sunday night, March 24, Edmund was brought back to the beloved Upland home.

Late Monday night, Elisabeth checked on him before she went to bed, adjusting the thermostat and Edmund's oxygen supply.

"Now rest good," Elisabeth told him. "You need to take a rest now, because you're so tired."

Edmund, still thinking of her, replied, "You need one, too."

That night Elisabeth couldn't sleep. She kept getting up to check on Edmund and make sure he had his oxygen. About five o'clock in the morning, when she got up to check again, she saw that only the earthly part of her husband still lay in the hospital bed. Edmund had reached the heavenly city at last.

At the funeral they played a song that had thrilled Elisabeth's heart at their wedding reception: *"So nimm denn meine Hände"* – "O Take My Hand, Dear Father." The Scripture reading and Gospel message were from Psalm 23. *"The Lord is my Shepherd; I shall not want..."* The Lord had been a faithful Shepherd to Edmund, leading and caring for him in green pastures and dark valleys. His goodness and mercy had followed Edmund all the days of his

*Edmund and Elisabeth at home in Upland.*

life, and now the Shepherd had taken his sheep home to dwell with Him forever.

The year after Edmund's death was the hardest of Elisabeth's life. The loss of the companionship that had sweetened her life for the last thirty-five years left a gaping hole. In frail health herself, she was unable to do much without exhaustion. She felt old and useless, unable to understand why God left her on earth when there was nothing that she could do.

"What then?" she asked herself while depression clutched at her. She reminded herself that she still had her children, her friends, her church family. "And that's all true," she said later, "but nobody can help you. You need to go through that alone. And I said, 'I have the Lord.'"

That key opened the door of Elisabeth's prison. She had the Lord. The One who brought her through so much had not left her now.

"I saw [a pastor] on the TV," Elisabeth said, "and he said, 'Jesus is enough.' And I say, is that not true? Jesus is enough; what do I need more? I need Him, and I can talk to Him in prayer. What can I do more? You know, we have so many people that I can pray for. That is not wrong that I am here. I thought, 'What should I *do* here?' Oh, but I can do *that*. I can go and remember people, and can pray and thank the Lord that He is so good."

And so Elisabeth began her unseen ministry of prayer. That hidden life of prayer, like an invisible, iridescent thread, causes her tapestry to shimmer with quiet beauty. In her little notebook, long lists of penciled names—friends, countries, world events—bear silent record to the work that Elisabeth does for her Lord. It is not easy work, that labor of prayer, but it is crucial, vital work.

Before Edmund passed away, he told Elisabeth to go to his brother Armin in Wisconsin.

Armin would take care of her. With much prayer, Elisabeth followed Edmund's advice. The Lord marvelously orchestrated the selling of the Upland home, and on December 31, 2012, Elisabeth moved to Brookfield.

Today she lives in a small apartment in an independent senior living center. Armin and Elisabeth live two miles away, and Armin's thoughtful care for his sister-in-law fully justifies his brother's confidence.

Living alone is no easier for Elisabeth now than it was in Eichenau. In fact, the limitations of age make it even harder. The Lord is still her comforter, and prayer is her great weapon. When depression tempts her in the quiet of her apartment, she walks the halls of the building and prays for the people behind each door.

At each window she stops to look out at the surrounding woods, hoping to catch a glimpse of her forest friends. Browsing deer, pudgy squirrels, rabbits, and red cardinals flit and roam outside the windows. Wild turkeys are Elisabeth's special delight. She knows their habits and haunts, and checks for them each morning. She says she never had as much time to stand and watch the animals as she does now, and she keenly enjoys her Lord's world of nature.

As in Szárazd, Germany, and Upland, Elisabeth is gathering friends around her in Brookfield. Almost everyone in the apartment complex knows and loves her. Her genuine care for each person she meets wins her friends wherever she goes. Elisabeth and three other ladies have an informal walking club, and the cheerful foursome is a common sight in the long halls.

Old friends are not forgotten, but are remembered with love and brought before the Lord in prayer.

Family is as dear as ever to Elisabeth. Both of her brothers have passed away, but she keeps in contact with her three children, her sister Kathi, and other relatives far and near. Loving phone calls fly between the little Brookfield apartment and family scattered all around the world.

Most of all, Elisabeth has her Lord. His love and companionship never fail, and in His word she continually finds new treasures. God promises His special care to the widow as surely as to the orphan, and Elisabeth is still proving Him absolutely faithful.

Elisabeth, too, is faithful. The Lord's thread is weaker now outwardly, but its inner strength is renewed day by day. Waiting, working, and watching for her Lord's return, she walks on in trust and beauty. The Lord is still weaving...

This story is dedicated to the Father of the fatherless, who faithfully kept His word to provide and care for four orphans:
Elisabeth, Hans, Heinrich, Kathi.

*A Father of the fatherless, and a judge of the widows, is God in his holy habitation.*
*Psalm 68:5*

*The LORD preserveth the strangers; he relieveth the fatherless and widow: but the way of the wicked he turneth upside down.*
*Psalm 146:9*

*He doth execute the judgment of the fatherless and widow, and loveth the stranger, in giving him food and raiment.*
*Deuteronomy 10:18*

# Bibliography

With many thanks to the editors of Wikipedia and Deutsche Wikipedia for compiling and making available historical resources that would otherwise have been difficult or impossible to find.

### History of Szárazd:

Wolf, Johann. *Chronik der ev. Luth. Gemeinde Szárazd im Komitat Tolna Ungarn.* 1993.

### History of the Blischke Family:

Schairer, Lydia. *Fleeing All but His Presence.* Waukesha, WI: Heritage Quality Instant Print., 1992.

### Deportations from Bessarabia:

Caşu, Igor (2010). "Stalinist Terror in Soviet Moldavia". In McDermott, Kevin; Stibbe, Matthew. *Stalinist Terror in Eastern Europe.* Manchester University Press.

### Deportations from Hungary:

Stark, Tamás. "Genocide or Genocidal Massacre?: The Case of Hungarian Prisoners in Soviet Custody." Human Rights Review. April–June *2000*, Volume 1, Issue 3, pp. 109-118.

Várdy, Agnes Huszár. "Forgotten Victims of World War II: Hungarian Women in Soviet Forced Labor Camps." Previously published in: S. B. Várdy - T.H. Tooley - A. H.

Várdy, *Ethnic Cleansing in Twentieth-Century Europe*, Columbia University Press, New York 2003, pp. 503-516.

Zielbauer, Gyorgy. "Magyar polgari lakosok deportalasa es hadifogsaga 1945-1948" (The Deportation and Captivity of Hungarian Civilians, 1945-1948), Tortenelmi Szemle 3-4 (1989): p. 289.

# Pronunciation Guide to Foreign Words and Phrases

| | |
|---|---|
| acacia | a-kah'-see-ah |
| Alsace | ahl-sahss' |
| auf wiedersehn | owf vee'-der-zane |
| bauer | bow'-er |
| Bayerisch | bie'-er-ish |
| Becht | bekt |
| Bessarabiendeutsche | bess-a-RAH'-bee-en-doi'-chuh |
| Blischke | blish'-kee |
| Danke Herr | dahn'-kə hair |
| Donaueschingen | doh-now-esh'-ing-en |
| Eichenau | ī'-ken-ow |
| Ének | ay'-nək |
| Felsőnána | fel-shə-nah'-na |
| fillér | halfway between fill-eer' and fill-air' |
| Frank | frahnk |
| frau | frow |
| fräulein | frow'-line |
| Girching | geer'-hing |
| halztuch | hahlz'-tookh |
| hanf | hahnf |
| Hauptstadt | haupt'-shtadt |
| hausfrau | hows'-frow |
| Heini | hie'-nee |
| Heinrich | hine'-rick |
| Ist kratzig | eest kraht'-seekh |
| Jakob | yah'-kəb |

jeles .................................................... yel'-esh

jó ............................................................. yoh

Jossip Monasterly................yoh'-seep moh-nast'-ter-ly

Jugend .............................................yoo'-gənd

Jungschar...................................... yung'-shar

kaffee-klatch ...........................kah'-fee-klatch

Kapos-Koppány...................kah'-pōsh-koh-pah'-ny

kaput ............................... kah-put', with "put" to
rhyme with "foot"

Katharina ................................ kaht-ah-ree'-nah

Kathi.....................................................kah'-thee

kitűnő .......................................kit'-uh-nurh

kleine küsse ...................klīn-ə kuis-ə"ui" pronounced
halfway between "oo" and "ih"

kuchen ......................................................koo'-khen

Künzing..............................kuin'-sing; "ui" pronounced
halfway between "oo" and "ih"

Leni .................. halfway between lay'-nee and len'-nee

Lepp.....................................................................lep

Lisje.........................................................liss'-ee-a

Ludwig Peter Walz ..................lood'-vikh pee'-ter vahlz

Maiglöckchen ....................... mie'-gluck-shen; "gluck"
to rhyme with "book"

mais ..............mah-ees; the "ah" and "ee" run together
into a single syllable

málenkij robot ...........................mah'-len-kee roh'-bət

Mathildendorf .........................................mah-till'-den-dorf

Münsingen ..................muin'-sing-ən; "ui" pronounced
halfway between "oo" and "ih"

Nagyvárad...................................nadj-vah'-rad

netzhaup................................................nets'-howp

nudeltuchen................................... noo'-dle-too-kən
oma ........................................................ oh'-mah
opa ......................................................... oh'-pah
Osterhofen ............................... ōs'-ter-hō-fən
Ostfront ...................................... ahst'-front
Paks ........................................................pahksh
paprika ...................................... pah'-pree-kah
paschke .................................................pahsh'-kə
pengő...................................................... pang'-uh
Renate......................................................rə-nah'-tə
riesling wein..............................rees'-ling vine
schnell .......................................................shnel
Schülerausweis .... shui'-ler-ows-vice; "ui" pronounced
                        halfway between "oo" and "ih."
Schwäbisch..................................... shvay'-bish
Sió ..............................................................shee-oh'
Stadtpfarrkirche.................... shtad'-far-kir-kuh
Szárazd .................................................sahr'-ahzd
Szekszárd.............................................sek'-zard
turnhalle ...................................... toorn'-hall-uh
Vilshofen..............................................vils-hō'-fen
visontlátásra ............................. vee-sohnt-lah'-tash-rah
Winecker ..........................................vin'-ə-ker
wurst.........................................................verst
Zwiefalten ............................... zvee-fahlt'-en

# Knitting Pattern for Traditional Szárazd Paschke

*Three sizes of paschke. Left to right: men's, women's, child's. The printed cloth in the background was Mother's from Hungary, and the white cloth is Father's handwoven hanf.*

Hand-knit *paschke* are Elisabeth's signature gift. Szárazd *paschke* are traditionally black, with brightly-colored roses embroidered on the toes. Elisabeth knits *paschke* in all colors, freely adapting the pattern for different sizes and yarns.

## Materials:
-3 oz. worsted weight yarn
-Set of 4 or 5 US size 1 double-pointed needles
-Size G crochet hook (for working edging)

Gauge: 7 stitches per inch.

Finished Size: Women's 5-6. Stitch counts for men's size 8-9 and children's size 7-8 (toddler) are given in parentheses following the women's stitch counts.

The pattern can easily be enlarged by using larger needles and/or yarn to increase the gauge. The women's pattern, knit with US size 5 double-pointed needles at a gauge of 5 stitches per inch, fits a men's size 9-11.

### Heel Section knitted on 2 needles in the flat:
Cast on 44 (52, 36) stitches.

**Row 1:** K44 (52, 36), turn.

**Row 2:** P2, K2, P across to last 4 sts, K2, P2, turn.

**Rows 3-18 (3-20, 3-12):** Repeat rows 1 and 2, ending with row 2.

### Heel Shaping (Short Row Heel):
**Row 1:** K28 (33, 23), SSK, turn.

**Row 2:** Slip first stitch, P12 (14, 10), P2tog, turn.

**Row 3:** Sl 1, K12 (14, 10), SSK, turn.

Repeat last two rows until all stitches have been worked, ending with a purlwise row.

### Body:
**Row 1:** Sl 1, K13, (15, 11) pick up and knit 10 (11,7) stitches, turn.

**Row 2**: P2, K2, P6 (7, 3), inc. P-wise (P, leaving st on needle, then slip same st K-wise), P13 (15, 11), pick up and P 10 (11, 7), turn.

**Row 3**: K2, P2, K6 (7, 3), inc. K-wise (K, leaving st on needle, then slip same st P-wise), K across, turn.

**Row 4**: P2, K2, P3 (3, 1), inc. P-wise, P across, turn.

**Row 5**: K2, P2, K3 (3, 1), inc. K-wise, K across, turn.

**Row 6**: P2, K2, P6 (7, 2), inc. P-wise, P across, turn.

**Row 7**: K2, P2, K6 (7, 2), inc. K-wise, K across, turn.

**\*For children's pattern, skip to row 12.**

**Row 8**: P2, K2, P2 (5), inc. P-wise, P across, turn.

**Row 9**: K2, P2, K2 (5), inc. K-wise, K across, turn.

**Row 10**: P2, K2, P6 (7), inc. P-wise, P across, turn.

**Row 11**: K2, P2, K6 (7), inc. K-wise, K across, turn.

**Row 12**: P2, K2, P across, turn.

**Row 13**: K2, P2, K across, turn.

**Rows 14-18 (14-24, 14-18)**: Repeat last two rows, ending with a purlwise row (add or remove rows here as needed).

**Row 19 (26, 19)**: K2, P2, K18 (20, 12). Place row marker. **\*For children's pattern, skip page 206.**

**Begin knitting in the round:**

**Row 1**: K15 (17), P1, K3, P1, K2, cast on 4 st, join; K2, P1, K3, P1, K around.

**Row 2**: K15 (17), P1, K3, P1, K8, P1, K3, P1, K around.

**Rows 3-12 (3-14)**: Repeat previous row (add or remove rows as needed).

## Toe Shaping:

### Men's pattern:
Work next two rows, then follow women's pattern.
**Row 1**: K10, K2tog, K2, SSK, K1, P1, K3, P1, K8, P1, K3, P1, K1, K2tog, K2, SSK, K around.
**Row 2**: K around to 1st P on prev row, P1, K3, P1, K8, P1, K3, P1, K around.
Move to row 1 of women's pattern.

### Women's pattern:
**Row 1**: K9, K2tog, K2, SSK, P1, K3, P1, K8, P1, K3, P1, K2tog, K2, SSK, K around.
**Row 2**: K around to 1st P on prev row, P1, K3, P1, K8, P1, K3, P1, K around.
**Row 3**: K around to last st before dec on 2nd row down, K2tog, K2, SSK, K to nxt P on prev row, P1, K8, P1, K to last st before dec, K2tog, K2, SSK, K around.
**Row 4**: K around to 1st P on prev row, P1, K8, P1, K around.
**Rows 5-10**: Repeat last 2 rows, ending with row 4.
**Row 11**: K around to last st before dec, K2tog, K2, SSK, K around to last st before dec, K2tog, K2, SSK, K around.
**Rows 12-15**: Repeat last row until only 8 sts remain.
**Row 16**: K2tog, SSK, K2tog, SSK; 4 sts remaining.
**Row 17**: K2tog, K2tog; 2 sts remaining.
Pull one st through the other, break yarn, draw yarn through loop. Work in ends.
Work edging around ankle opening (see next page).

## Edging for men's or boys' paschke:

**Row 1**: Single crochet into every other knit stitch around, join with slip stitch to first sc.

**Row 2**: Chain 1, sc in same st, sc in each sc around, join with sl st to first sc; finish off.

## Edging for women's or girls' paschke:

**Row 1**: Single crochet into every other knit stitch around, join with slip stitch to first sc.

**Row 2**: Chain 1, * skip nxt sc, (sc, ch3, sc) in nxt sc,* around, join last ch3 with sl st to 1st sc, finish off.

## Children's Pattern (cont. from page 203):

**Begin knitting in the round:**
**Row 1**: K15, P2, K1, cast on 4 st, join; K1, P2, K around.
**Row 2**: K15, P2, K6, P2, K around.
**Rows 3-9**: Repeat previous row (add or remove rows as needed).

**Toe Shaping:**
**Row 1**: K8, K2tog, K2, SSK, K1, P2, K6, P2, K2tog, K2, SSK, K around.
**Row 2**: K around to 1st P on prev row, P2, K6, P2, K around.
**Row 3**: K around to last st before dec on 2nd row down, K2tog, K2, SSK, P2, K6, P2, K2tog, K2, SSK, K around.
**Row 4**: K around to 1st P on prev row, P2, K6, P2, K around.
**Row 5**: K around to last st before dec on 2nd row down, K2tog, K2, SSK, P1, K6, P1, K2tog, K2, SSK, K around.
**Row 6**: K around to 1st P on prev row, P1, K6, P1, K around.
**Row 7**: K around to last st before dec, K2tog, K2, SSK, K around to last st before dec, K2tog, K2, SSK, K around.
Repeat last row until only 8 sts remain.
Dec around; 4 sts remaining.
Dec twice; 2 sts remaining.

Pull one st through the other, break yarn, draw yarn through loop. Work in ends.

Work edging around ankle opening (see page 205).

## Stitch Abbreviations:

### Knitting:
dec – decrease
inc. – increase
K – knit
K2tog – knit two together
K-wise – knitwise
nxt – next
P – purl
prev – previous
P-wise – purlwise
S – slip
SSK – slip-slip-knit
st – stitch
sts – stitches

### Crocheting:
ch – chain
sc – single crochet
sl st – slip stitch

Pattern may be copied for personal use.

# Mother's "Kleine Küsse" Cookies

**Mother's Original Recipe:**

12 egg whites
400 g ground walnuts
250 g powdered sugar

Beat egg whites very stiff, then stir in walnuts and sugar. Bake in preheated oven at 350°-375.°

Mother's recipe is deceptively simple. Only three ingredients followed by brief instructions, but I found I couldn't reproduce the white "little kisses" that Elisabeth described. No matter how small I made the cookies, they always browned before they were done in the center. Elisabeth was too young to remember how long her mother baked them, but said you had to *watch* them to make sure they didn't cook too long. The cookies were dried after baking, she remembered, but didn't know whether Mother dried them in the oven or not. I experimented with different baking and drying times and found that, though not authentic, following a recipe for meringues gave the best results.

A note at the top of Mother's recipe said *"Halb."* At first I thought that was the name of the recipe, but later Elisabeth told me it was simply a note to make only half a recipe. 12 egg whites makes a huge number of cookies.

In Hungary tiny peppermint candies decorated the top of the *kleine küsse*. Crushed peppermints can be used instead.

## Updated Recipe:

6 egg whites
200 g (about 1 7/8 cups) ground walnuts
125 g (about 1 1/4 cups) powdered sugar
Tiny peppermint candies, or crushed peppermints, for topping (optional)

Preheat oven to 200.° Beat egg whites very stiff, then slowly beat in powdered sugar until mixture is stiff and glossy. Carefully fold in walnuts. Drop by teaspoonfuls on a lined cookie sheet. Bake for 2 1/2 hours.

# About the Author

Emily Potter lives with her family in Altadena, California, in the foothills of the San Gabriel Mountains. She has loved words and languages since she was a child, and enjoys the challenge of finding just the right word for each situation. Emily loves spending time with family and friends, talking about the Lord and His work, and enjoying the beauty of God's handiwork in nature. Sewing, reading, studying Mandarin Chinese, and playing with her two little nephews are some of her favorite pastimes. Her greatest joy is walking with her Lord each day, and she asks for prayer that she may "walk worthy of His calling" in His strength, having His will as her own.

Emily would love to hear stories of the Lord's work through this book in the lives of those who read it (along with better baking methods for *kleine küsse)*.

She can be contacted at:
emilypotter@seekyee.com

Or at:
Emily Potter
136 Wapello St.
Altadena, CA 91001
USA